D0258708

Greenwich Readers

Education & Training for Life

Planning Teaching
and
Assessing Learning

This Reader is one of a series designed to support teachers and trainers in the post-compulsory sector of education. It will be of value to those who are working in colleges of further and higher education, sixth form colleges, adult and community education institutes, training units, and institutions of specific vocational preparation in the health service, the police service and the armed forces. The topics have been selected to represent a wide view of currently important issues and, by providing appropriate material for critical reflection on professional practice, the book will meet the needs of experienced teachers and trainers as well as those in the earlier stages of their careers.

In addition to such general use, the volume is one component of an integrated Certificate in Education/Postgraduate Certificate in Education course offered by the School of Post-Compulsory Education and Training at the University of Greenwich. Further information on this and other programmes of study and related academic services may be obtained from:

School of PCET
University of Greenwich
30 Park Row
London SE10 9LS

telephone: 020 8331 9230
fax: 020 8331 9235
e-mail: pcet@gre.ac.uk
www.gre.ac.uk

The planned range of titles in this series is as follows:

- Adult Learners, Key Skills & the Post-16 Curriculum
- Equality, Participation & Inclusive Learning
- Flexible Learning & ICT

- Language, Communication & Learning
- Perspectives on Learning
- Planning Teaching & Assessing Learning
- Professionalism, Policies & Values
- Supporting Students

Enquiries about the current availability of these publications should be addressed to the School Office at the above address.

Tony Lewis
Series Editor

ACCESSION No: 029044

CLASS NUMBER: 371·3 COX

Planning Teaching
and
Assessing Learning

A Reader

Anne Cox
&
Harriet Harper

Selection, arrangement and introduction © University of Greenwich 2000.

All rights reserved. Except as permitted under current legislation, no part of this work may be photocopied, stored in a retrieval system, published, adapted, transmitted, recorded or reproduced in any form or by any means, without the prior permission of the copyright holder. Enquiries should be addressed to the University of Greenwich.

Published in 2000 by Greenwich University Press and prepared for publication by:

Procurement and Business Services Department
University of Greenwich
Woolwich University Campus
Wellington Street
London SE18 6PF

ISBN 1 86166 073 1

Cover designed by Pete Birkett

Text design and layout by Christine Murray

In the majority of cases the contents of the readings and extracts in this volume have been reproduced as they appear in the publications from which they have been taken.

Every effort has been made to trace all the copyright holders, but if any have inadvertently been overlooked the publishers will be pleased to make the necessary arrangements at the earliest opportunity.

University of Greenwich, a charity and a company limited by guarantee, registered in England (reg no 986729). Registered Office: 30 Park Row, Greenwich, London SE10 9LS.

Contents

Acknowledgements

Acknowledgement is made for permission to reproduce the extracts and diagrams quoted:

Brown S & Knight P (1994) *Assessing learners in higher education* Kogan Page, diagram from p46

Gibbs G, Habeshaw S & Habeshaw T (1988) *53 interesting ways to assess your students* 2nd edn Technical & Educational Services Ltd, pp77-79 and p115

Habeshaw S, Habeshaw T & Gibbs G (1992) *53 interesting things to do in your seminars and tutorials* Technical & Educational Services Ltd, pp17-19; pp23-24; pp63-64; p79

Minton D (1997) *Teaching skills in further and adult education* 2nd edn Macmillan, diagram from p117

Open University (1997) *Adult learners, education and training (E827) Project and assignment guide* The Open University

Race P (1993) *Never mind the teaching feel the learning* Paper 80 Staff and Educational Development Association, diagrams from pp42-43

Reece I & Walker S (1997) *Teaching, training and learning* 3rd edn Business Education, pp110-111; pp312-314; fig 6.5 from p375

Rogers A (1996) *Teaching adults* 2nd edn Open University Press, p129

Our thanks are also due to colleagues who provided material, in particular Michael Bloor, Julia Burton, Barbara Chandler, Maude Gould, Tom Ralph and Edwin Webb.

The School of Post-Compulsory Education and Training

The School of PCET, as it is known, has its origin in Garnett College in London, one of three institutions set up by the Ministry of Education in the late 1940s for the initial training of technical college lecturers. After many developments and organisational changes over the past 50 years, its future within the University of Greenwich will now be from a campus on the banks of the River Thames in Christopher Wren's former Royal Naval College.

The School's services and students, though, are not only locally based, but nationwide and international. PCET is a leader in distance provision for lecturers, trainers, administrators and other support staff from all sectors of post-school provision, as well as from the public services and voluntary and commercial training organisations. It has associated centres in various parts of the United Kingdom, and there are projects in China, South Africa and Russia, and leadership of research and information networks within the European Union.

We aim, in both our teaching and our research, to relate professional practice to learning theory and current policy issues. This permeates all of the School's programmes – from initial training on Certificate in Education/PGCE programmes, through professional development at BA/BSc and Masters levels and the work of our Training and Development Office, to our portfolio of short courses and bespoke in-house provision. There is a thriving group of research students, and the School has been at the forefront of innovation in computer mediated communication. We provide a comprehensive service for further, higher and adult education, helping people to help others learn through life.

Ian McNay
Head of School

Anne Cox worked as a computer programmer and a college lecturer before becoming involved in teacher education. She is a Senior Lecturer in the School of PCET at the University of Greenwich and currently pathway leader for the full-time PGCE/Certificate in Education. Her research interests include mentoring in further and higher education.

Harriet Harper taught a wide range of subjects, including Russian, English as a Second Language, Business Studies and Management, before specialising in Information Technology and becoming Head of a Business Computing Department in a further education college. She now works as an inspector in the college sector and as a tutor at the University of Greenwich, where her responsibilities include organising consultancy and professional development workshops for staff in further and higher education.

Introduction

The purpose of this text is to examine a number of fundamental issues concerning the planning and delivery of teaching and the assessment of learning in the post-school sector of education and training.

A brief preliminary part (*Overview* – Section 1) gives a survey of processes of learning and selected models of teaching, outlines the distinction between them and argues for a variety of approaches to the management and assessment of student learning and achievement.

The main body of the text is then divided into three further parts.

Part Two (*Programme Planning* – Section 2) looks at the wider context of the individual lesson by identifying and describing the factors that need to be considered when setting up a series of classes or training sessions, constructing an overall programme or scheme of work, and devising effective ways of planning initial and final tutorial meetings.

Part Three (*Lesson Preparation* – Sections 3–5) considers more closely and in more detail the specific issues concerned with how one particular lesson or training session can be planned, delivered and evaluated. It sets out to try to answer the following questions:

- what do we need to take into account when constructing a plan for an individual lesson?

- what strategies and resources for teaching and learning are available to the teacher or trainer, and in what situations might they best be used?

- what factors help us to communicate effectively and manage the interaction within tutorial groups?

- how can a lesson or training session be designed to meet the needs of a range of students within one group?

- what procedures can a tutor or trainer use to measure the effectiveness of a particular session, and thus plan to improve?

Part Four (*Assessment of Learning* – Sections 6–10) explores key issues relating to the assessment of learning. The questions considered here are:

- why do we need to assess?
- what do we assess?
- what types of assessment can we use?
- who is involved in the assessment process?
- how fair can we make assessment?
- how should we go about assessing?

Planning and preparing lessons is probably the most important single aspect of the work of the professional teacher/trainer. Having a well-thought-out structure for a lesson, or framework for a series of lessons, enables you to concentrate on showing and sharing your enthusiasm for the subject, on establishing productive relationships with your students and on managing interesting and challenging experiences that will help students learn. Assessing fairly the achievement of the learners in your classes is a central concern for all involved in teaching and training, and this influences many of the planning and delivery decisions made by teachers. Issues of equity, therefore, are considered at different points in the text.

The brief extracts which are incorporated into several of the sections have been taken from some of the standard textbooks in the field. A complete list of all books and articles referred to will be found at the end.

Throughout the text the terms *tutor, teacher* and *trainer* are used interchangeably. Similarly, no significant distinction is made between the words *learner, student* or *trainee*.

Anne Cox & Harriet Harper
April 2000

Part One – Overview

This overview will start by examining what is meant by the terms *learning, teaching* and *assessment,* and will go on to discuss briefly a number of different perspectives on the task of the teacher.

- Learning has been defined as a 'relatively permanent change in behaviour as a result of experience, training or practice' (Reece & Walker, 1997: 249). As teachers and trainers we hope that the knowledge, attitudes and/or skills of our students and trainees will be changed in some anticipated way as a result of the experiences and materials that we devise for them.

- Teaching is therefore usually defined in relation to learning. For example, Curzon describes teaching as 'a system of activities intended to induce learning' (Curzon, 1997: 21). It is the deliberate and planned nature of teaching that differentiates its results from other forms of incidental learning, though we do need to recognise that our teaching often has unintended consequences.

- Assessment links the two, by determining how far teaching has resulted in learning. As Derek Rowntree puts it: '... assessment tells you what and how well your students have learned' (Rowntree, 1981: 178). This draws attention to the close relationship between what we do and what our students do, and the need to take responsibility for whether they learn from us or not.

So it is important to recognise that the process of teaching consists of a set of conscious and premeditated activities where teacher and learner interact: it is not just a single one-way operation. Teaching is also to be distinguished from what we might call 'indoctrination': learning must take place more or less willingly and through morally acceptable means.

It is also useful for all of us who earn our living as teachers to remember that most of what people learn in life manages to happen without the intervention of any formal teaching at all.

1. Learning, Teaching and Assessing

This section briefly introduces the four principal issues that teachers and trainers will need to consider as they begin the process of planning and checking the learning of others.

- The first concerns the nature of what is to be learnt, that is the kind of learning that is expected to take place. Is it to be simply the memorising of facts and information; or a deeper comprehension of processes or relationships; or the acquisition of competence; or the justifying or changing of opinions; or the questioning and adjustment of personal conduct; or – most usually – some combination of these? Teachers and trainers need to know how the differences between types of learning will affect the planning of learning experiences.

- The second concerns the assumptions made by the teachers and trainers about the role that they play in facilitating students' learning. We can identify at least two 'models' of the teacher's role – the teacher as a 'broadcaster of knowledge', and the teacher as a 'manager of student learning'. Many planning decisions depend on the teacher's perception of the appropriateness of these roles in different circumstances.

- The third concerns how and how far it is possible to determine whether or not the intended learning has taken place, and to decide what are the proper and appropriate instruments that are needed in order to carry out such assessment of learning.

- The fourth concerns the teacher's wish to discover what might be done better next time round – the necessity to evaluate what has been happening and plan the next cycle of learning on the basis of that evaluation.

The nature of learning

Alan Rogers provides a five-fold classification of types of learning, drawing attention to the familiar distinction between:

- Knowledge
- Understanding
- Skills
- Attitudes
- Behaviour.

He indicates the importance of being able to discriminate between these different 'arenas' or 'spheres' of learning in the following way:

1) *We may learn new* **knowledge** *as we collect information that is largely memorised.*

2) *Such knowledge may be held uncomprehendingly. Thus we need to learn to relate our new material in ways that lead to new* **understanding**, *that*

3

process of organising and reorganising knowledge to create new patterns of relationships.

3) *We may learn new **skills** or develop existing skills further; not just physical skills, our ability to do certain things, but also skills of thinking and of learning, skills of coping and solving problems and survival strategies.*

4) *Further, since we can learn new knowledge, new understanding and new skills without necessarily changing our attitudes, the learning of **attitudes** is a distinct sphere of learning.*

5) *Finally, it is possible for learning changes to be brought about in all four of these areas without accompanying alterations in our way of life, our pattern of **behaviour**. It is therefore necessary to learn to apply our newly learned material to what we do and how we live, to carry out our new learning into changed ways of behaving: what some people would call to learn 'wisdom', in short.*

(Rogers, 1996: 129)

While it is true that most learning experiences represent a complex interaction between two or more of these five areas, it is helpful for teachers to be able to distinguish between them. This is because different approaches to the planning of teaching may be appropriate in the different 'spheres'.

For example, sessions which are intended to help learners memorise vocabulary in a foreign language or formulae in mathematics may need to be taught in one way, while sessions which aim to change attitudes towards disability in the workplace will need quite a different approach. In other words, decisions made during the planning stage with regard to the selection of teaching methods will, in part, be determined by the nature of the content or subject matter and which 'sphere' or combination of spheres it falls within.

Role of the teacher in facilitating learning

Effective teachers and trainers create an environment in which students/trainees can learn. To do this, they must plan carefully, build productive relationships with students, and monitor and learn from the progress the students make. There are different views or models of the teacher's role in the classroom. Two contrasting perspectives are presented here: the teacher as a 'broadcaster' of knowledge, and the teacher as a 'manager' of student learning.

These models may be used to help us to examine critically the decisions that we and our colleagues take when planning and delivering a lesson, and an awareness of them can make it possible for us to establish a framework for evaluating the effectiveness of a particular session.

Model 1: The teacher as broadcaster of knowledge (the transmission model)

A simple model of a one-way, linear relationship between teaching and learning might look like this:

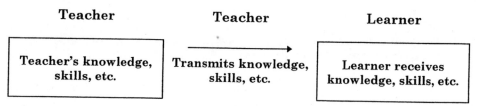

Figure 1   The transmission model

This is sometimes referred to as the 'traditional' model of teaching. It presents an image of a teacher in front of the class delivering information to more-or-less passive students. This model suggests that teaching is a matter of simply organising the knowledge, skills and attitudes that the teacher possesses, and handing them over to the students.

Though there may be many occasions when this is an appropriate way to pass on information, there are a number of problems with this model. Teaching, like other forms of communication, is a two-way process. Students do not simply absorb ideas; they try to build up meanings in their own heads, based partly on what the teacher is presenting, and partly on what they already know.

Often these meanings are those the teacher intended, and sometimes they are not. For example, teachers may use technical terms that are understood by some students and not by others; some of the group may already have a knowledge of the topic, others not.

There are further factors that influence learners which are not reflected in this model. Motivation, for example: some of the learners may have a positive attitude towards the subject, others may associate it with negative feelings – perhaps with fear or boredom experienced at school. The age, ethnicity, gender of the students will also affect how they perceive and interpret information.

The next model takes such complexities into account.

Model 2: The teacher as manager of student learning (the interactive model)

This model presents a more interactive view of teaching and learning. The students interact with the teacher and with each other, with the teacher's knowledge of the subject, with their own previous experiences, and with the demands of the course or programme.

The process is very different from the transmission model of instruction. It is a view of teaching and learning which recognises that teachers have to be aware of many different aspects of their students' experiences. They must consider not only *what* is to be taught, but also *how* it will be taught, and to *whom*. Teachers need to concern themselves with what the students already know, and their attitudes to the subject, to the teacher and to other members of the learning group.

If we accept this alternative model, we shall see teaching as:

... a process of working co-operatively with learners to help them change their understanding. It is making student learning possible. Teaching involves finding out about student misunderstandings, intervening to change them and creating a context of learning which encourages students actively to engage with the subject matter.

(Ramsden, 1992: 114)

Students may have misunderstood previous lessons on the topic or on related subjects; they may have more experience or less as students; they may have a preference for a particular way of learning. Age, gender, ethnicity or particular learning needs will influence their approaches to learning, and the teacher has to take all of these factors into account when planning and delivering a lesson.

The planning of lessons, therefore, requires teachers to make a link between their own experience and knowledge and the students' needs and previous experiences.

Figure 2 shows this diagrammatically.

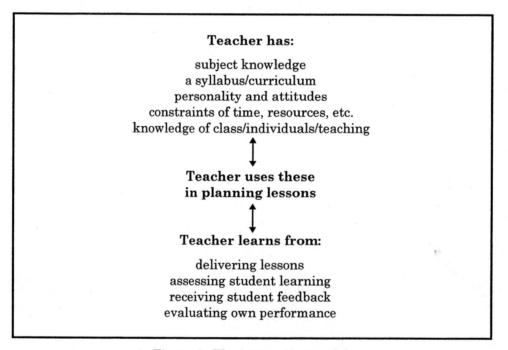

Teacher has:

subject knowledge
a syllabus/curriculum
personality and attitudes
constraints of time, resources, etc.
knowledge of class/individuals/teaching

**Teacher uses these
in planning lessons**

Teacher learns from:

delivering lessons
assessing student learning
receiving student feedback
evaluating own performance

Figure 2   The interactive model

As managers of student learning, teachers need also to be adaptable and responsive to their students during the progress of a lesson; this means that they have to develop ways of assessing learning and thus of measuring the effectiveness of their sessions.

Approaches to the assessment of learning

Assessment strategies have to be planned just as teaching methods have to be planned. Teachers and trainers must have an understanding of the purpose of assessment, a knowledge of the types of assessment at their disposal, and a clear perception of what constitutes an assessment scheme that is fair to the learners.

The evaluative cycle

Finally, it is important to remember that lesson planning is part of a cycle which involves the teacher in evaluating how effective a session or a programme has been, thinking about how it could be improved, changing the plan and – more often than not – delivering the (amended) plan again. This cyclical process is important, whether applied to a single, one-off lesson/training session, or to a complete scheme of work for a week, a whole term or a year.

Figure 3 is a reminder that plans are not static: they need to be developed in the light of experience.

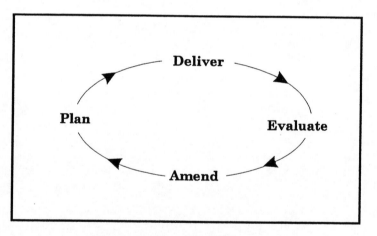

Figure 3   The evaluative cycle

The experience of identifying the strengths and areas for improvement in one session helps planning in other contexts; in other words, it contributes to a teacher's overall development in planning, delivering and assessing learning.

Part Two – Programme Planning

Teachers who work in colleges are likely to be familiar with schemes of work. These show in outline the sequence of teaching intentions for a whole unit, course or programme of study. In training organisations, such intentions are more often indicated by a set of training proposals.

In Figure 2 (page 6) we identified some of the characteristics and constraints which teachers and trainers may bring to the planning of individual lessons.

These apply no less to the development of complete courses and programmes of study; indeed, because of the longer time scales involved, the activities of planning, structuring and sequencing are even more crucial. Chief among these activities is what Derek Rowntree calls 'the structure of events' – an identification of the 'key events or critical happenings ... marking the closing and opening of different phases within the course' (Rowntree, 1981: 94). A scheme of work is the public statement of this structure.

For trainers in commercial and industrial contexts, this public statement may take a different form. It is often known as a training proposal, and such a document usually summarises the events and intended outcomes of a training programme. This could be seen as an informal contract between the trainer and the participant in a training event (or with the employer when a freelance trainer works with a company). A training proposal will, like a scheme of work, indicate time-scales and the different phases of a course; however, unlike a scheme of work, it may show the intentions for a single day or half day (whereas schemes of work usually show a set of regular meetings over a term or a year). In addition to this, they may form an important part of the publicity materials for a course or conference, and indeed the market research may have been at a much more intense level than for most college educational programmes.

The essential characteristics of both schemes of work and training proposals are that:

- they give an overview of the course, possibly indicating the pre-requisite knowledge, skills or experience required of participants, together with an indication of the assessment requirements;

- they show the sequence of topics, often incorporating a time-scale of events;

- they form part of the communication between lecturers and students, or trainers and trainees.

2. Schemes of Work and Training Proposals

This section examines in detail the format of schemes of work and training proposals, and gives an indication of how they can best be designed. Some of the factors which influence the sequencing of topics are identified, and the planning of sessions which are particularly important to the overall scheme or proposal – namely the first and last sessions of a course and the building of relationships with a new group of learners – are also covered.

Producing a scheme of work

A scheme of work (sometimes identified as a sequence of topics, or a training programme proposal) presents the overall plan for a series of lessons or training sessions. Ian Reece and Stephen Walker describe a scheme of work as: 'a series of planned learning experiences sequenced to achieve the course aim in the most effective way' (Reece & Walker, 1997: 315).

At all stages in the planning of teaching, it is important to try to provide variety for the learners. Some teachers provide a great deal of detail on the scheme of work: an indication of teaching/learning strategies, resources etc. might be included, and this can help in checking that there is a balance of different approaches and activities over a whole course or throughout a whole day.

In some institutions, schemes of work are produced collectively by a course team. This is most common where there are a number of parallel classes running in a college – for example, GCSE English or Mathematics, or GNVQ in Business and Finance. A similar situation occurs in the context of training when large numbers of staff have to learn about new aspects of their duties at the same or similar times – for example, IT training when a new Management Information System is being introduced. In these situations, an agreed scheme helps to ensure consistency and enables students to transfer from one class or group to another if necessary. More commonly, individual teachers will produce their own schemes of work; however, some courses require co-ordination between different subjects, and teachers often need to develop their schemes in conjunction with the colleagues responsible for these other subjects. This is the case on GNVQ/NVQ programmes where collaboration is needed to ensure that there is appropriate coverage of key skills, and on many business studies and management training schemes, where skills and knowledge from one area (e.g. statistics) are used by another (e.g. marketing).

Schemes of work are generally produced from the course aims, using the teacher's knowledge of the subject and of the groups to be taught, the time allowed, the resources available, and the assessment requirements of the course. Although schemes of work can take different forms, they usually show the date of the session (or equivalent, such as a week number), the topic to be covered (often with some indication of detailed content), the sequencing of topics, and the assessment tasks examination dates).

11

A typical scheme of work for seven weekly one-day sessions for a group of adults studying basic skills could look something like Figure 4. Notice how the scheme begins with an overview and diagnostic session, and how each week has a theme or topic associated with it and an indication of the broad assessment tasks for each week.

Week	Topic	Assessment
1	*Introduction.* Overview of the aims of the course; getting to know each other (ice breaker). Review of work done before the course. Applications of numeracy in business and other real life situations. Research for next week.	Activity: what have you done before the course?
2	*Measuring and weighing.* Litres, millilitres, kilograms, grams. Weighing and measuring activities in pairs. Data gathering exercise for next week.	Diaries: weighing and measuring
3	*Working with calculators.* Using them with confidence to add, subtract, multiply and divide.	Calculator worksheet
4	*Shopping around for bargains.* Value for money in the supermarket (addition, subtraction, multiplication, division).	'Best Buy' worksheet
5	*Working with percentages.* What is a percentage? Calculating percentage (50%, 10%, 5%). Calculating a discount.	Role play and worksheet
6	*Conversion.* Litres and pints, pounds and kilograms.	Revision
7	*Assessment Week.* Individual work.	Red Café case study

Figure 4 Scheme of work for numeracy class for adults

The scheme of work forms an important part of the documentation for any course. Students should always be given a copy of the scheme, and many teachers use the first meeting with a class to discuss the plan for the course.

The complete process is shown in the following diagram:

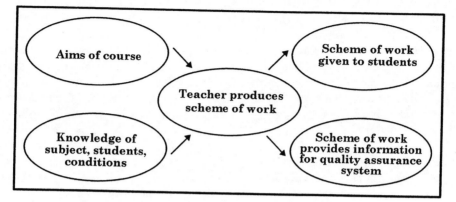

Figure 5   Information flow

In institutional settings, the teacher is usually required to provide a copy for the unit or subject leader as part of college quality procedures; copies may also need to be made available for external verifiers or examiners, and for inspectors.

Designing a training proposal

Training proposals are usually drawn up by in-house training advisers or by an external training consultant. The training outcomes may emerge from a process of identifying any gaps between the current skills/knowledge levels of individuals within the organisation and the requirements of the company. The mode of delivery – face-to-face, formal group work, off-the-job training, one-to-one coaching etc. – will normally be negotiated with the training manager.

It is important to bear in mind that organisations do not stand still, and a vital aspect of such a training needs analysis is to compare the current level of expertise with the skills that the organisation will need in the future.

The stages in designing a training proposal are thus:

1. identify the performance objectives required;
2. carry out an audit of existing skills and knowledge;
3. draw up a *training needs analysis* to identify discrepancies between people's current capabilities and what is required in the future;
4. formulate training proposals (training objectives and training design).

In the first stage, the organisation's current and future needs must be identified. Senior management may have already recognised these, or this may be part of an external consultant's job.

For example, if a company is planning to move into new markets in Germany, the training consultant may be required to identify the skills and knowledge required by the office staff in order to cope with this change.

The next stage would be to identify the existing level of expertise in the German language within the company. Members of staff with German skills need to be located.

Thirdly, the consultant should establish an individual's language competence and knowledge of German business practices and customs in detail, and then, by matching this against the performance objectives, identify that individual's training needs. For example, a German speaker, competent in speaking informally in face-to-face situations, might need training to enable them to talk on the telephone, using business vocabulary.

The final stage is to use this information to formulate a training proposal; this may be a proposal for an individual, as in this example, or for a group or whole department, when new procedures or IT equipment and software is introduced.

In some cases, these stages will not proceed as smoothly as this summary suggests. It is possible that other relevant training needs will be discovered that have been overlooked in the initial formulation of performance objectives – perhaps the audit might reveal relevant suggestions from the employees being assessed. For example, the German-speaking employees might identify colleagues with language experience who would benefit from training in German, or they might suggest further relevant skills such as formal written business communication in German, or some appreciation of relevant European legislation. Often, it will be important to consider these suggestions, and this may mean that parts of the audit and parts of the training needs analysis will be reconsidered, or extended to include other employees.

Methods of collecting information

If the needs of the organisation have not yet been established, the consultant might do this by interviewing managers, possibly in combination with routine staff appraisal interviews. Auditing staff members' existing skills is usually done by questionnaire, semi-structured interviews or by direct observation. Semi-structured interviews usually contain a number of prepared questions (prompts) followed by supplementary questions which encourage the interviewee to answer the question in more depth (probes).

There are a number of advantages and disadvantages associated with all these approaches. Questionnaires are inexpensive to distribute, and can be completed in privacy and at a time convenient to the respondents; but they reveal only the skills and knowledge that members of staff are themselves aware of and it is hard to design questions that are clear and unambiguous. Semi-structured interviews enable questions to be clarified and the interviewer can adapt to the interviewee, but they are expensive in terms of staff time.

An alternative to using questionnaires and interviews is to watch and listen to people, but observation is expensive, and does not reveal information about situations that will arise in the future (see, for example, the company planning to move into new markets described above).

The way in which the information is collected will affect the accuracy of the picture of the employees' training needs presented. If employees in the German-speaking example above complete a questionnaire which asks them about how well they can deal with a business telephone conversation conducted in German, they may try to answer as accurately as possible. However, their responses may be influenced (consciously or unconsciously) by factors such as low self-esteem (which may make them underestimate their skills), or fear of losing their jobs (which may make them overestimate their abilities).

Even methods that rely on observation, which might overcome these problems, may introduce other factors which affect the accuracy of the data. For example, employees' performance may be affected by the presence of the observer, and will vary naturally from day to day. In addition different observers may interpret what they see differently: it must be in a form that will give information that is detailed enough to establish an individual's training requirements.

Training proposals

The resulting set of training proposals may often take the form of a scheme of work, but more commonly they will incorporate more precise timings, particularly when they represent the activities to be carried out on a one-day training event or conference. The publication of a detailed timetable is often a part of the marketing and advance documentation of the course. It is also very likely that the usual work or business environment of such an occasion will impose its own need to be exact about the structure of the day, as participants – whether from the providing organisation or not – will have certain expectations about how their own individual needs will be met. Purposes and anticipated outcomes will probably have to be more exactly and realistically expressed, and value-for-money or rate-of-return-on-investment considerations are likely to be high on the list of priorities in the minds of those who may have paid a significant fee (both in money and in opportunity costs) in order to attend. The end-of-programme review or conference evaluation is an important part of the day.

In the example which follows we see that it has the timings which are characteristic of most lesson plans, while indicating the purpose of each session and the periods of time allocated to the important activity of socialising during the refreshment breaks. This gives the participants an opportunity to influence the course of events during the day and to establish, in a way, their own agenda. The formal activities demonstrate a variety of approaches, which will allow individual, small group and whole group learning. The sequence of topics will also have been worked out with some care.

The scheme of work or training proposal will often show more than just the sequence of topics. While it will not be as detailed as an individual lesson plan, it may additionally include an indication of teaching/learning strategies, assessment methods, and resources; it is likely also to give an indication of procedures for feed-back and evaluation.

	Title: Time Management in the Workplace – a one-day course	
Time	**Topic / Activity**	**Notes**
9.30	*Coffee and registration*	
9.45	Introduction. How to become really organised: beat the top time wasters.	This will give participants an overview of the most common time wasters in the office and how to deal with them – including fine tuning your 'to do' list; establishing priorities etc.
10.15	Dealing with everyday jobs efficiently.	An exercise that will help you make the best use of your day.
10.45	*Coffee*	
11.00	Handling paperwork.	Strategies to create time and save money.
11.20	Don't put it off!	Overcome procrastination by using our tips and techniques: some activities and resources that will help you.
12.00	Plenary: review of the morning sessions.	To consolidate what you have learnt and prepare for the afternoon session.
12.30	*Lunch*	A selection of our training resources will be on display and available for purchase.
1.30	First things first.	Goal setting and prioritising: workshops in small groups.
2.30	Harmony and perspective.	Achieving balance in your working life: putting it all together; action planning.
3.30	*Tea* and closing plenary.	Evaluation of day – an opportunity for you to tell us what you found useful and what you would like in the future.

Figure 6   Training proposal for a one-day course

However, a statement of the order of topics or activities will be the most important feature of any programme plan, and there are a number of ways of doing this.

Justification for sequencing

The sequencing of topics will depend partly on the logical requirements of the subject itself (and for some subjects, such as mathematics, there is less freedom to sequence topics in different ways than in others), partly on the needs of the students and partly on the preferences of the teacher. Ian Reece and Stephen Walker offer the following suggestions:

Sequence of Topics

The sequence of topics is often derived from a syllabus or list of issues to be taught. There are, however, several ways in which you can establish your order of teaching. Some of these are:

1. **Easiest topics first** ... in this way you can gain the confidence of students before addressing the more difficult issues.

2. **A theme** ... some courses can be seen in terms of themes and two or more themes make up the scheme of work; for example Parliament: theme, elections.

3. **Logical sequence** ... in mathematics there is a need to learn addition and subtraction before multiplication and division, so it is logical to have that sequence.

4. **Begin with the topics that you as the teacher are familiar with** ... you may be in the position of being familiar only with part of the syllabus, and teaching what you know allows you time to prepare the other topics.

5. **Historical/ chronological order** ... the causes of the First World War are taught before the battles – this is a logical and natural order; however, if you start the teaching with a major battle and its effects, you might create impact and the interest to see the causes.

6. **Normal/abnormal** ... start with the normal situation and move toward the abnormal or unusual.

7. **Seasonal** ... many topics are influenced by the seasons, e.g. cooking – availability of vegetables, horticulture – particular tasks are related to the time of year.

8. **Anatomical** ... start at the feet and move up towards the head.

9. **Fear/apprehension** ... with an antenatal class, first-time mums are concerned about labour pains – so deal with this first.

10. **Sensitivity** ... if dealing with a healthy lifestyle, perhaps smoking should be one of the final issues – otherwise students may leave early in the course!

11. **Most helpful** ... if your students' course is related to their work, then start with topics which are most relevant to them, hence creating maximum impact.

12. **Controversial** ... starting with the least/most controversial topic may be important.

13. **Theory/practice** ... you may wish to integrate/mix theoretical issues with the practice or may wish to keep them discrete.

Continued...

14. Geographical	... this may be a useful way to link social issues or natural resources.
15. Negotiation	... set out the issues and agree a sequence with the student.
16. Availability	... of resources such as guest speakers, video, workshop, laboratory, computers.
17. Group confidence development	... in order to discuss sensitive issues, e.g. child abuse, or to use challenging teaching strategies, e.g. role play.
18. Demands of other subjects	... scientific or technological subjects may need to be preceded by certain mathematical topics.
19. Opportunistic	... responding to the latest political news as part of the lesson on politics, applying plaster cast in the icy season.
20. Must know, should know, could know	... many syllabuses are overcrowded so the essential topics are addressed, then the next more important and so on; for example, with a driving and car ownership course:

Must know
know position of controls
switch on and start engine
change gear and brake
drive in a safe manner
Should know
check oil and water levels
change wheel
check tyre pressure
Could know
change light bulbs
change windscreen wiper

21. Order of the textbook	... textbooks are rarely written with sequence of teaching in mind.
22. Safety	... health and safety concerns may dictate certain issues are addressed at a very early stage in the course.
23. Evaluation	... previous cohorts when evaluating the course may suggest a different sequence of topics.

(Reece & Walker, 1997: 312–314)

The students' attitudes towards the subject, and their mode of attendance (full-time, part-time, distance/flexible) may well influence the decisions on sequencing. A group of students with a history of failure in a subject could require an approach which incorporates 'easiest topics first...', while others who enjoy debate and argument may respond well to 'controversial topics first...'. The major themes may be laid down in textbooks or flexible learning materials, and planners might find it helpful to adopt the same themes in order to support students in part-time or flexible attendance modes.

Arranging topics in a course is not always straightforward, even after the main reasons for sequencing (e.g. logical order plus group confidence) have been decided. Reece & Walker go on to offer some practical advice:

Step 1 Identify all the topics to be covered, the length of time you estimate it would take to teach and assess each of them, and the importance of the topic within the overall course (see point 20 in the extract above).

Step 2 Write the title of each topic on an individual card and number them, in no particular order (e.g. topic A, topic B, topic C etc.)

Step 3 Now use these cards to sort the topics into order, taking into consideration any of the principles in the above extract which are relevant, but particularly:
- is there a relationship between the topic on one card and the topic on another?
- if so, must one of the topics be learnt before the other?

This can become complicated, especially if the sequence of topics seems to satisfy one of the planner's aims (e.g. logical ordering) but not another (e.g. group confidence).

In whatever way the topics are ordered, it is important for the planner to be able to explain the reasons for the chosen sequence.

After the sequence of topics has been decided, the time has come to prepare the individual sessions in detail, through the construction of a series of lesson plans. But before we deal with these, in the next section, we will look at the important business of planning the first and the last lesson in a course or series of lessons.

Planning the first session

This first session can be used to establish trust and an atmosphere of psychological safety. It is also an opportunity to establish and agree a set of operating principles, or 'ground rules'. Habeshaw, Habeshaw & Gibbs (1992) and Nugent (1996) make several suggestions about how to start off with a new group. These include: strategies for getting to know the members of the group, starting to learn participants' names and, if they do not already know each other, ideas for helping them become acquainted. These 'icebreakers' can be done individually, in pairs or in small groups, and should include the teacher/trainer.

Getting to Know You

The sooner members of your tutorial group get to know each other, the sooner they will feel easy about working together and participating in discussion. If you spend some time on introductory exercises at the beginning of a course, students will feel that they have made a start in getting to know each other.

There are three sorts of exercise you can do: individual, in pairs, in small groups. (Whichever you do, don't forget to join in yourself.)

Continued...

---

a) Individual

Each person introduces herself and says something about herself. It's helpful if you make explicit what this should be and write it on the board.

It could be:
- my name
- where I'm from, and
- why I'm here
or
- my name
- which options I'm doing, and
- who else I know in this room.

b) Pairs

Group members get into pairs and spend three minutes each finding out about their partner. At the end of the six minutes, each person introduces her partner to the rest of the group and tells them something about her.

c) Small groups

Students form groups of three or four and spend five minutes finding out what they've got in common with the others in their group: taste in music, 'A' levels, Auntie Annies, and so on. At the end of five minutes they report to the other groups what they have in common.

One advantage of this type of exercise is that it ensures that everybody has the experience of speaking early on. If you want your students to get used to speaking in tutorials, the sooner they start the better.

If individuals join your tutorial group late, don't forget to organise introductions for them.

You could say, for example, 'This is Chris, who's transferred from another course. I'd like to welcome you to this group. Who do you know here? ... Perhaps the rest of you would like to tell Chris who you are and say something about yourselves. (I'll draw a plan of the room with the names on, Chris, to help you remember who everyone is.) And then we'll ask you to say something about yourself. OK, who'd like to start?'

(Habeshaw, Habeshaw & Gibbs, 1992: 17–18)

The exact nature of the activities should take into account the age, composition, previous learning and general level of sophistication of the participants, as ill-chosen 'games' with the wrong group of people can have the exact opposite of the intended effect.

Nugent sums up his position in the following way: 'At the first meeting I believe students need to feel welcome, to feel safe, to feel a sense of belonging' (Nugent, 1996: 19–20).

He carries out two sorts of activities:

1) *Welcome and introductions*: he says a little about himself, asks students to introduce themselves (perhaps saying what they expect to get from the course), checks that everyone knows each other's names, remembers that different cultures have different conventions for meeting and greeting, and establishes the ground rules for working together.

2) *Information sharing*: this involves giving an outline of the course and finding out how familiar students are with the subject/topic; he then clarifies details of assessment and evaluation, giving details about the institution and perhaps talking about his preference for a teaching style that requires a co-operative learning environment, so that students should feel free to question what they're learning and how; in addition, he indicates that he likes to start and finish on time.

These activities at the beginning of a course can act as icebreakers, and they also enable the teacher to tell the students about the course content, and to discuss the processes involved. In the example above, Nugent uses the opportunity to give a preview of the course which will help the students to prepare for learning. He also gives the group some important messages about his intended teaching and learning strategies, about how he wishes the students to interact with each other and with him, and how he sees his own contribution to and the students' roles in the learning process.

An effective opening session, therefore, might include an overview of the course and an opportunity for the tutor begin to establish relationships by learning the students' names and establishing ground rules. Suggestions for strategies for the learning of names and the establishing of ground rules will now be considered in greater detail.

Students' names

To function really effectively as a teacher, it is important to know students' names; members of a group need to know everyone else's names, too, if they are to work well together. If the group participants already know each other, but this is the first time the teacher has worked with them, it is still worth checking that they remember each other's names. Students can use name badges or put cards with their names in front of them on the table; or the learning of names can be part of an activity.

Habeshaw, Habeshaw & Gibbs make the following recommendations:

If you have started with some kind of introductory exercise, they will already have heard each other's names. You can build on this in the following ways:

a) *Get students in turn to say the names of everyone in the group and join in yourself. Then change places and do it again until all the names are familiar.*

b) *On the board draw a plan of the furniture in the room and as students speak, write in each name at the appropriate point on the plan.*

21

c) *Ask students to say their own name first when they speak in the group for the first few times and when they form pairs ask them to remind their partner of their name.*

d) *Encourage them to ask when they forget someone's name.*

e) *Use students' names yourself when you speak to them.*

Students sometimes find the activities potentially embarrassing but often remark later how quickly the group gelled as a result.

(Habeshaw, Habeshaw & Gibbs, 1992: 19)

As we have already noted, there are rules, assumptions and conventions which govern the activities of all groups; these are usually unspoken and often unquestioned. When these rules and conventions work well, individuals feel comfortable and are able to make contributions without fearing embarrassment. However, if the conventions do not suit all the members of the group, there may be times when students feel uneasy. In extreme situations there may even be conflict generated within the group. This is likely to be an important consideration when participants differ widely in age and/or educational experience.

It is therefore sensible to establish ground rules that make explicit the assumptions about acceptable behaviour and that indicate the teacher's expectation that conventions should be agreed and open to negotiation. This will help to provide both the teacher/trainer and the group with strategies for avoiding friction, or with procedures for coping with conflict if it arises.

If possible, this discussion should be held with the group during its first meeting, as it is important to involve the group in establishing these rules. Habeshaw, Habeshaw & Gibbs recommend taking positive steps to specify and agree 'ways of working together'.

Ground Rules

Students who are unused to setting their own ground rules may find it difficult at first to see what you mean and will be wary of making suggestions. They may find it helpful if you take the activity in two stages:

- first explain the principle of ground rules and together make a preliminary list;
- then, after one or more tutorials, ask them, in the light of their experience, what changes they would like to make to the list.

Their list could look something like this:

Ground rules for this group:

a) No smoking except in coffee breaks.
b) Don't interrupt other people.

Continued...

---

c) It's OK to opt out and opt in again.

d) Anyone can suggest changing or adding to the ground rules at any time.

e) Every group member is entitled to time.

f) It's OK to ask other people for help.

g) At any point anyone can suggest that the group moves on.

h) We start on the hour and finish at ten minutes to.

The best way of ensuring that the ground rules are kept is for group members to be scrupulous from the outset about reminding people when they break them.

It is important that you as a teacher don't see yourself as being above the law; you should encourage students to remind you if you break a ground rule and accept the reminder when they do.

(Habeshaw, Habeshaw & Gibbs, 1992: 23–24)

Planning the final session

The last session is sometimes given over entirely to looking back – evaluating the course (see Section 5, below) and identifying any unfinished business. This may be combined with a celebration of success/achievement of goals, and looking forward to the next part of the course or sharing individual plans for the future. Sometimes, group members appreciate the opportunity to make more personal farewells. Ideas for encouraging this include:

- having an end of year party;
- asking students to write a note to other individuals in the group saying one thing they have appreciated about being in a group with them;
- asking students to tell the other members of the group what they have valued most about the experience of doing that unit.

Where individuals work one-to-one with the teacher, these approaches need to be adapted; some tutors take the opportunity to offer feedback to the student to reinforce the progress the student has made.

Planning a learning programme or series of lessons provides the framework for the next stage: planning individual lessons in detail. Sometimes, it may be necessary to return to the overall scheme once the planning for individual lessons has been completed, and this is one of the reasons why all the plans for a programme of study need to be considered before it starts, so that adjustments can be made to the scheme before it is distributed to the students. In the next section, we will discuss the process of lesson planning in detail.

Part Three – Lesson Preparation

Planning every teaching or training session requires thinking about a great variety of different factors. In earlier sections it has been suggested that the planning of teaching includes thinking about students and teachers interacting with each other. Planning a lesson, therefore, involves more than organising the content into digestible chunks. Teachers will need to think about the learners' previous experiences and disposition towards learning, the changes that will take place in terms of the learners' knowledge, skills and attitudes, the environment in which this will take place (and this may be a classroom, the workplace or a virtual setting), the time involved, and the choice of teaching and assessment methods.

These aspects of planning are encapsulated by David Minton, who suggests that lecturers and trainers should begin their lesson planning by asking themselves the following questions:

1) *Who* am I going to teach?

2) *What* are they going to learn?

3) *Where* are they going to learn, or where am I going to teach?

4) *When and how long* is each teaching session?

5) *How* am I going to teach them, and how will I know what they have learnt?

(Adapted from Minton, 1997: 46–47)

In addition to this, teachers will need to devise plans for judging how effective the session has been. This involves looking at the results of an assessment task in order to ascertain the success of the learning; but it should also offer learners opportunities to provide the teacher with their views on how effective they feel the experience has been. Often this is done through written or verbal feedback at the end of a programme of study, but it should be done informally at more regular intervals throughout the course in order to help the teacher respond quickly to the learners' needs and to maintain their involvement in the evaluative cycle described on page 7.

3.   Planning a Lesson

This section deals with writing lesson plans. In practice, these 'plans' may take many different forms, because they will represent many different 'lessons' in a variety of contexts, e.g.

- *a conventional class*, that is a group of students or trainees learning in a classroom setting in a college or commercial organisation;

- *one-to-one teaching* in the workplace or college, in an art and design workshop, in a library where learning support is provided, or in an IT or science laboratory;

- *supporting flexible learning*, where students follow information and activities presented in printed learning materials or interact with Information and Communication Technology (ICT) based materials.

Plans for these distinct contexts will have their own typical characteristics, but they will all attempt to answer Minton's five questions: Who? What? Where? When? How?

The first example is for a 'conventional' class, and will be discussed in some detail. Further on in the section, there are examples of plans for one-to-one teaching, and for supporting flexible learning.

Lesson Plans

A lesson plan, then, indicates the teacher's answers to such questions as are posed by Minton. We have already indicated that teaching is a *planned* activity, and drawing up a plan before each lesson forces tutors to clarify their intentions, their choice of teaching methods, their plans for assessment, and any materials which they might use. Lesson plans should contain enough information to act as a prompt during the session; detailed information on content is kept for the tutor's subject notes. (This set of content notes, remember, does *not* constitute a lesson plan.)

The plan, together with the subsequent lesson evaluation, forms an important part of the record of the session. Such records, like schemes of work and training proposals, are increasingly required for audit and quality procedures inside institutions and by external verifiers, visitors, examiners and inspectors.

There are numerous ways of indicating what your intentions are for a forthcoming teaching or training session, but they are all expected to have certain features in common, and they are best set out in a clear and consistent way. Many colleges or departments have a standard two-sided proforma which they ask their staff to use.

On the following pages a lesson plan has been completed, using such a form, for Week 5 of the scheme of work which was presented in Figure 4 (page 12 above). The first page, by and large, answers Minton's questions; the second page outlines the structure, sequence and timing of the lesson. At the end of the first page will be found some 'notes on differentiation', that is an indication of how the plan will accommodate learners with a range of needs; more details on this will be found in then final column of the second page.

Lesson Plan

Date: *4th March*　　　　　**Time:** *13.00*　　　　　**Duration:** *2 hours*

College site & room: *Northwood, Room 31*

Course: *Adult Basic Skills*　　　　**Subject:** *Numeracy Workshop: Week 5*

No. of students: *15*　　　　**Topic:** *Working with percentages*

Lesson aims:
To introduce percentages and how to calculate and use them

Specific learning outcomes:
Students will be able to:
1. understand the meaning of percentage
2. calculate simple percentages on paper
3. calculate percentages using a calculator
4. use percentages in the calculation of discounted prices

Previous knowledge assumed:
Students can add, subtract, multiply and divide
Students can use the basic functions on a calculator

Materials and equipment required:
Handouts. Worksheets. Role-play guidelines
Whiteboard and pens. Overhead projector (OHP)
Calculators

Assessment method:
Discussion and question & answer (Q&A)
Completion of handouts
Worksheet tasks
Role-play in pairs – shopkeeper and customer

Homework:
Calculate further discounts on handouts

Notes on differentiation and equal opportunities:
All students will be given assistance with their worksheets when necessary, and open-ended tasks will provide activities for those working at a faster pace.
Role-play to be designed so that all can participate.
Versions of all printed materials in large font are available for the visually-impaired member of the group. This student will be seated in an appropriate position when the whiteboard or screen is used.

Figure 7　Completed lesson plan

Time/ Stage	Subject Matter or Content	Activity: Teacher	Students	Resources & Notes (and differentiation)
1.00 Intro	Welcome students; take register; give overview of session.	VE (Verbal exposition) Q&A.	Q&A (Question & answer).	Whiteboard. (Check seating for visually-impaired student)
1.05	Link to last lesson; check knowledge of application of percentages.	Q&A.	Q&A. take notes.	Note points on board. (Check all students able to participate)
1.10 Develop't	Discuss application of percentages.	VE, Q&A.	Q&A.	Handout: food labels & contents.
1.15	How to calculate percentages.	VE, Q&A and demo.	Listen, Q&A take notes.	OHT & Handout.
1.25	Worksheet.	Monitor & assist. VE & demo.	Individual work.	Worksheet 1. (Help students as needed)
1.40	Review work, show correct method & lead discussion.	Demo	Listen, Q&A.	Whiteboard. (Check all students able to participate)
1.50	How to calculate discount.	VE, Q&A, and demo.	Listen, Q&A.	OHT & Handout.
2.00	Worksheet.	Monitor & assist.	Work in pairs.	Worksheet 2. (Help students as needed)
2.20	Review work, show correct method and lead discussion.	VE & demo.	Listen, Q&A.	Whiteboard.
2.30	Briefing for roles: shopkeeper, customer, observer.	VE, Q&A.	Q&A.	Divide into threes; arrange seating; distribute briefing. (All students must be able to take part in this)
2.35	Role-play exercise.	Check, help and assess.	Role-play.	
2.50	Role-play debriefing.	Note key points on whiteboard.	Q&A, take notes.	Whiteboard. (Encouragement given to less confident students)
2.55 Conclusion	Recap on session; check points needing further work; set home work and link to next lesson.	VE, Q&A.	Q&A, take notes.	OHT and home-work handout. (Further work & home-work focused on individual student needs)

Figure 8   Completed lesson structure/content proforma

The decisions that the teacher has made and recorded in the specimen lesson plan are quite complex. If we look back at page 25 we can expand and apply Minton's five categories of question to this document and see how far it will help us to understand why lesson plans are important.

1. Who?

The first set of decisions concerns the students. Planning means, amongst other things, knowing about the skills and knowledge which they already possess and which they need in order to profit from the lesson. This information indicates the general expected state of 'readiness' of the students, and is entered on the plan under the heading 'previous knowledge assumed':

> **Previous knowledge assumed:**
>
> *Students can add, subtract, multiply and divide.*
>
> *Students can use the basic functions on a calculator.*

However, students will not often all be in the same state of readiness, and planning has to take the needs of individual learners into account. In the Numeracy lesson plan, we noted that this has been covered on both of the two pages. First (Figure 7), the teacher has considered the range of needs within the group and how the plan can be made to suit all of the members. This may have implications for materials (as it does in this example).

> **Notes on differentiation and equal opportunities:**
>
> *All students will be given assistance with their worksheets when necessary, and open-ended tasks will provide activities for those working at a faster pace.*
> *Role-play to be designed so that all can participate.*
> *Versions of all printed materials in large font are available for the visually-impaired member of the group. This student will be seated in an appropriate position when the whiteboard or screen is used.*

The teacher will also need to consider in detail how these different needs can be met at successive stages of the lesson. This is shown in the final column of Figure 8, and is indicated in our example by the use of brackets.

Here, the teacher has planned each activity within the lesson in turn, and considered how each phase can be managed in order to accommodate the needs of the range of learners within the group. As in many cases, the plan must offer both support to more hesitant learners and at the same time relevant challenges for the quicker workers.

So there are a number of individual characteristics of the learners which will need to be considered at the planning stage. In the example above, the fact that some students are expected to complete the tasks more quickly than others may be as a result of previous experience, previous levels of attainment, motivation or self-confidence. Other factors such as age, ethnic and social background, gender, attitudes (to the topic, the teacher and the rest of the group), or special needs might affect students' requirements.

When thinking about these factors, teachers must be careful to remember not to label their students (for example, not all older students lack confidence) but to base their judgements on what they really know about the individuals concerned. In some contexts, colleagues can provide relevant information about learners' attitudes, motivation and needs; in other situations, the trainer must find these things out from the students themselves. David Minton offers this comment:

> *[Students] do know about themselves, which you [the teacher] do not. Most people will welcome the chance to talk about themselves and what they feel they need. Teachers often report that their students were grateful and welcomed the opportunity to talk to a teacher 'who wanted to know about me'. This is the critical starting point of a process of building up a spirit of trust between students and teacher.*

(Minton, 1997: 47)

These factors do not always appear on a lesson plan, but they should influence the choice of teaching and learning strategies. Sometimes, a tutor will wish to choose methods that will keep the chances of disruptive behaviour to a minimum. The issue of student behaviour is dealt with later on in this section.

2. What?

The next set of decisions concerns the content. First, we need to look at the teaching aims and the learning outcomes (or objectives) in order to complete the first part of the lesson plan.

Aims express the main purposes of the lesson. They are *teaching* goals, and are expressed in terms of what the teacher is planning to do for the students. Aims can be expressed at different levels: overall course aims, subject (or unit) aims and individual lesson aims; it is important to bear in mind the course aims/unit aims when writing lesson aims. The aims on a lesson plan should describe the teacher's or the course's intentions. Week 5 in the Numeracy Workshop has the following aims: *'To introduce percentages and how to calculate and use them.'*

Aims of other lessons might typically be:

- to introduce cost/benefit analysis
- to explore the uses of the Internet in marketing
- to develop bread-making skills
- to review the use of imagery in Shakespeare's sonnets
- to develop the skills necessary to work safely with scientific apparatus
- to build students' confidence in their interview skills.

Learning outcomes are much more specific, and have been defined as 'statements of what a learner can do, know and understand as a result of learning' (UDACE, 1992).

If teachers describe content in this way, it helps them focus on what the learner should achieve rather than what the lesson should contain; this approach is consistent with tutors seeing themselves as managers of student learning, rather than as transmitters of knowledge. It prepares the teacher to communicate these intentions clearly and precisely to students (and any others concerned, such as employers). Another advantage is that the link between the teacher's intentions and the assessment of student learning can be made much clearer.

In the case of the Numeracy Workshop, four learning outcomes are given. These are expressed in terms of what the students are expected to be able to understand and do:

Specific learning outcomes:

Students will be able to:
1. *understand the meaning of percentage*
2. *calculate simple percentages on paper*
3. *calculate percentages using a calculator*
4. *use percentages in the calculation of discounted prices*

The simplest way to write a learning outcome is to begin with a phrase such as 'students/trainees/learners will be able to ...' followed by a verb which suggests action (identify, analyse, recall, etc). The conditions under which the action is to be performed are also often stated.

Further examples of learning outcomes are:

Students will be able to:

*   open a bottle of wine correctly
*   deal constructively with customer complaints about faulty goods
*   write a report for a sales manager using appropriate language
*   compare the effect of using water colour, gouache and acrylic in a landscape painting
*   describe the difference between meiosis and mitosis in cell division
*   answer a business telephone call, using appropriate French vocabulary
*   compose and send an email message to a colleague about a future meeting
*   purchase a drink in the canteen with confidence.

These examples demonstrate the distinction we made in Section 1 between different kinds of learning. Learning is conventionally divided into three different categories or 'domains', expressed simply as:

*   knowing things (knowledge, the *cognitive* domain)
*   feeling things (attitudes, the *affective* domain)
*   doing things (skills, the *psychomotor* domain).

Some outcomes combine learning from all domains. For a student with learning difficulties, for example, buying a drink in the canteen may draw on all three domains: knowing the way that coinage is used; feeling confident enough to approach the counter; being able to count out the appropriate coins.

The examples of verbs in Appendix A give an indication of the variety of ways in which we can express learning outcomes.

3. Where?

On the Adult Basic Skills lesson plan only the room number is shown. However, there are other details about the environment that should be considered.

- What is the arrangement of desks/tables and chairs in the room?
- Can these be moved around?
- Where is the whiteboard? Can it be seen easily by everyone in the room?
- Is there an OHP? Is there access to IT facilities?
- What are the acoustics like? If possible avoid asking: 'Can you hear me at the back?' – try to find this out before you start teaching.
- At the time you will be teaching, will the room be light/warm/cool enough?

These questions can be answered easily enough if the room is a familiar one; if not, it may be necessary to check it before completing the lesson plan.

4. When?

The time of the lesson will affect planning decisions. Some classes take place in the evening after work, some immediately after lunch when learners can be at their least attentive. The teacher should bear this in mind when planning. And most of all, the length of the lesson, over which few teachers have any control, must be adhered to; other teachers may be waiting for the room, or the students, and it is professionally discourteous to keep them waiting.

5. How?

There are important decisions to be made about how appropriate teaching/learning strategies might be chosen, the structure within which these will be used, and how the effectiveness of these will be judged in terms of the quality of student learning.

Some general points will be covered in this section; other issues relating to particular media and methods will be considered in Section 4.

Structure

A lesson can be usefully thought of as having three phases or stages:

1. Introduction to the lesson
2. Development
3. Conclusion.

The proforma in Figure 8 indicates these three stages, in the left-hand column.

Introduction to the lesson:

As we have seen, the beginning of a lesson can be carried out in a variety of ways. It might include the following:

- greeting the students and making them feel welcome;

- giving an overview of the lesson: the aims, the outcomes, what activities are going to be included, how learning will be assessed;

- making some links with the previous lesson, perhaps a summary of what has gone before;

- using an activity or questioning to provide some checks on the knowledge/ previous experience of the students.

Question and answer is an effective way of making contact with the students at the start of a lesson, and this is dealt with in more detail in Section 4. Some teachers like to begin a lesson in a more dramatic way with a story or brief case-study, or posing a problem to engage the students' attention.

Development

In this phase, it is important to choose a variety of strategies to keep the learners actively engaged and enable them to learn in different ways. This should provide a balance between student-centred and teacher-led activities, and will help the tutor to make provision for the differences in students' needs. Lessons might typically include:

- *a demonstration* where the students are shown how to perform a task (kneading dough, sketching a graph, drawing up a balance sheet, emboldening text), followed by students practising this skill with the tutor's support;

- *an explanation of an idea* (the function of a raising agent, the gradient of a straight line), followed by students working on the application of this idea;

- *a background survey* of legislation concerning racial discrimination, followed by a role-play to explore the attitudes surrounding discrimination in the workplace;

- *a problem-solving task* on marketing goods, followed by a tutor-led discussion which draws out theoretical issues;

- *the study of flexible learning materials* on designing questionnaires, followed by a task which requires the student to criticise an example of a questionnaire;

- *the formation of individual responses* to a poem following guidelines on a handout, then working in small groups to synthesise these responses and present to the whole class.

In these examples, teacher-centred methods are followed by student-centred ones. Information is presented by the teacher, either orally or through the use of guidelines or task sheets, and the students then apply what has been learned to the understanding of rules and principles. This combination of strategies encourages learners to engage actively and confidently with the material and information.

Sometimes it is appropriate to reverse this order – the class might begin with a role-play, draw points of principle out from the experience, and then relate this to legislation. These two ways of presenting new material are sometimes called *inductive* and *deductive* approaches. An inductive approach to learning is when the students begin by examining a number of examples, and from this identify generalisations, principles or rules. In a deductive approach, the learning begins with generalisations, rules or principles, and then these are illustrated through examples.

Reece & Walker use the teaching of magnetism to illustrate the difference between these two approaches.

Inductive and Deductive Approaches

Suppose we wished our students to gain an understanding of magnetic forces. We could give the students a magnet and a number of items made from a range of different materials. The students are then allowed to explore the use of the magnet and the various items made from the different materials. The students may then list items attracted to magnets and those not attracted. You may have to prompt this stage. The list may be as follows:

Attracted by magnet	Not attracted by magnet
pen	plastic pen
chair leg	paper
watch	cup
paper clip	wood
hair clip	clothes
spoon	
zip	

You can then ask the students to make a statement which summarizes their observations. It may be that they say metals are attracted by the magnet. A more sophisticated test would indicate only some metals are attracted by the magnet. The students can then be given more objects and asked to predict which items would be attracted.

An alternative approach would be to give out magnets, telling the students that magnets attract (some) metals but not objects made from other materials. Question and answer could then be used to ask the students to predict, then test, whether the magnets will attract various materials.

The two methods have some commonality. Essentially the content and equipment are the same. Both methods depend upon the generalisation that magnets attract (some) metals. However there are significant differences. In the first case the students make observations about specific examples and then make and test a general statement.

Continued...

This process of moving from specific examples to a generalised statement – or law – is called an *inductive* approach and would be advocated by humanists. In the second case the generalization was stated and then tested using specific examples. This process of working from a general statement and using specific examples is known as a *deductive* approach and would be advocated by behaviourists.

Both approaches have their benefits, and choice of approach may depend upon the topic under consideration. Also some students in your class will prefer an inductive approach whilst the other students may learn better with the deductive one.

It could well be that the best approach is to use a mix of the two throughout the course.

(Reece & Walker, 1997: 110–111)

Conclusion

This will need to be planned carefully, and is as crucial as the opening and the development phases. It is important to remember to leave enough time on the plan to manage the conclusion!

The following items might be included in this phase:

- review of the content of the lesson, emphasising the key points;

- feedback to the class;

- evaluation of the session and feedback *from* the class on how the lesson went;

- linking of this lesson to the next lesson, or to another part of the course;

- negotiation with the students time to allow them to clear away (portfolios, lab equipment, utensils), save computer files, etc;

- setting homework or work to be done before next session.

All of the decisions are recorded on the second page of the lesson plan. The example lesson has been planned in this way, and these three stages are indicated on the structure/content proforma.

Assessment

The next question is, 'How will you know what the students have learnt?' Assessing learning is a continuous process, not just something that happens at the end of unit or course. Assessment tasks provide feedback for the learners and for the tutor (a warm feeling that a class seems to have 'gone well' doesn't reliably tell the teacher that learning has occurred!). Assessment is part of learning, too. Writing essays and solving problems, for example, help the students to practise the skills involved.

The methods of assessment for the lesson should be indicated on the plan. This is the entry from the lesson on percentages:

Assessment method:

1. *Discussion and question and answer (Q&A)*
2. *Completion of handouts*
3. *Worksheet tasks*
4. *Role-play in pairs – shopkeeper and customer*

It can be seen here how the methods of assessment chosen match the learning outcomes. Sometimes, written tasks are appropriate (as in the example 'plan for skills associated with percentages'). For other categories of outcome (beating egg whites, decorating a vase) observing the performance or judging the look of a finished product is appropriate.

A common way of checking on students' learning during a lesson is the question and answer (Q&A) technique, though it is worth remembering that it rarely gives information about all the class members.

Planning for 'drop in' sessions

A great deal of teaching is not class-based, though, and teachers may be required to help students who present themselves at one-to-one sessions of various kinds: study skills lessons, drop-in workshops, individual support on key skills, academic tutorials, etc. In these sessions it is more difficult, in the conventional sense, to plan in advance.

Usually students have themselves identified a problem. This may be quite specific: for example, in an IT workshop they may not know how to create a table using a word-processing package. On other occasions, the need may be more complex and require a longer term solution: for example, the student may have poor study skills or lack motivation.

In situations like these, teachers need an approach which will provide some structure for their response to the students' requests. It is helpful to think of these encounters as mini lessons, with a beginning (a diagnostic phase), a middle (a development phase) and an end (a conclusion).

The following two plans show examples of such one-to-one sessions. The first plan (Figures 9 and 10) is for a student who has made an appointment with the tutor for support in dealing with a recurring problem, the correct use of the apostrophe in written English.

Lesson Plan

Date: *4th July*   **Time:** *16.30*   **Duration:** *20 mins*

College site & room: *Tutorial Room*

Course: *Learning Support*   **Subject:** *Key Skills*

No. of students: *One*   **Topic:** *Use of the apostrophe*

Lesson aims:

> *To establish the use and functions of the apostrophe*

Specific learning outcomes:

> *Student will be able to:*
>
> > *1. recognise when the apostrophe is used in abbreviations*
> >
> > *2. recall how it is used with a possessive 's'*
> >
> > *3. distinguish between these two functions*
> >
> > *4. write out phrases and sentences using the apostrophe correctly*

Previous knowledge assumed:

> *Student knows the difference between apostrophes and inverted commas*

Materials and equipment required:

> *Examples of student's own written work*

Assessment method:

> *Listening and question & answer (Q&A)*
> *Completion of practice tasks*
> *Correction of own written work*

Homework:

> *Further practice, if appropriate, in preparation for a follow-up meeting*

Notes on differentiation and equal opportunities:

The student's individual needs will be further assessed during the meeting.
Tutor will develop tasks appropriate for the individual, based on the student's responses during the session.
Any follow-up work set will reinforce learning or challenge the student to extend learning as appropriate.

Figure 9   Completed lesson plan for one-to-one learning support session

Time/ Stage	Subject Matter or Content	Activity: Teacher	Student	Resources & Notes (and differentiation)
16.30 Diagnosis	Greet student and review written work to find errors.	Listen and contribute.	Read text and identify errors.	Student's script.
16.33	Categorise examples into 'missing letter' rule and 'possession' rule.	Listen.	Explain, take notes.	(All activities designed to suit individual student)
16.35 Develop't	Add to list of examples.	Prompt.	Record.	
16.40	If all apostrophes are misunderstood, teach 'missing letter' rule and work through examples from text, from student, & from teacher suggestions. If 'missing letter' rule is understood, but the 'possession' rule is not, work out rule from examples from work. Teach rule, and practise.	Observe & contribute.	Explain and question. Contribute examples.	
	Decide on strategy: eliminate apostrophes, except 'missing letter' use, OR only put in apostrophes that the student can explain.	Discuss.	Discuss.	
16.48 Conclusion	Work to be done for next appointment. Agree time.	Set work.	Agree task.	

Figure 10   Completed lesson structure/content proforma for one-to-one learning support session

In the second example (Figures 11 and 12) the tutor is planning a telephone tutorial with a student following a degree course delivered in flexible learning mode.

Lesson Plan

Date: *28th May*   **Time:** *13.00*   **Duration:** *20-30 mins*

College site & room: *Telephone tutorial, from home*

Course: *BA programme*   **Subject:** *Research Methods (flexible learning)*

No. of students: *1*   **Topic:** *Questionnaire Design*

Lesson aims:

> *To investigate the student's understanding of:*
> > *the circumstances under which a Qre would be used to collect data*
> > *factors to be taken into account in the design of Qres*

Specific learning outcomes:

> *By the end of this part of the course the student will be able to:*
> > *1. identify the circumstances under which a Qre would be used*
> > *2. describe the advantages & disadvantages of using Qres*
> > *3. outline the implications for data analysis and interpretation*
> > *4. evaluate an example Qre by commenting critically on aspects of the general design, and on the questions themselves*
> > *5. design a revised Qre, taking into account points raised above*

Previous knowledge assumed:

> *The student will have read the section in the course materials relating to Qre design and begun to engage with the task associated with this topic; two or three issues for discussion will have been identified before the tutorial.*

Materials and equipment required:

> *Both student and tutor will have copies of the course materials to hand*

Assessment method:

> *Discussion and question & answer (Q&A)*

Homework:

> *A formative written task to be submitted after the telephone tutorial*

Notes on differentiation and equal opportunities:

Tutor will assess needs and develop relevant tasks during the encounter; follow-up work will reinforce learning or challenge student to extend learning as appropriate.

Figure 11   Completed lesson plan for telephone tutorial

Time/ Stage	Subject Matter or Content	Activity: Teacher	Student	Resources & Notes (and differentiation)
1.00 Diagnosis	Usual greetings. Review of progress to date.	Ask student to identify specific issues to be discussed.	Raise 2 or 3 issues arising from the materials.	Course materials, and draft of student's preliminary work on the task.
1.05 Develop't	Exploration of student's understanding of topics.	VE, Q&A.	Q&A.	(Tutor will know of any study issues that might arise.)
1.15	Clarification of issues.	VE, Q&A.	Listen, Q&A.	(Care will be taken throughout to use voice to compensate for lack of visual contact with student.)
1.20 Conclusion	Identify action plan: tasks in the materials which will reinforce learning and extend it.	Agree plan and arrange next phone call.		

Figure 12 Completed lesson structure/content proforma for telephone tutorial

This type of encounter, where the tutor responds to the student's needs as they are identified, occurs in face-to-face teaching as well as with distance learners. It is vital in all tutorials of this kind, where the learning outcomes are agreed during the interaction, that the tutor devises a method of recording the student's learning and action plan. If the student had agreed the topic to be discussed with the tutor beforehand (perhaps via email) the lesson plan would have been more specific, and would be similar to the plan for learning support (see Figures 9 and 10).

In each of the above two examples the three-stage structure of a lesson is maintained, though amended in the way we suggested earlier.

Diagnostic phase:

The tutor uses question and answer or observation or a check-list to identify and clarify the learning need, and to check the student's existing skills and knowledge. It is important for the tutor to remain alert to problems and lack of understanding that the student may be unaware of, even at undergraduate level. The tutor has to be able to establish a positive relationship quickly, and to ensure that the student feels safe. This is a particularly important skill when tutor and student do not meet face to face.

Development phase:

The tutor will have to choose an appropriate teaching strategy, or negotiate an approach, that will suit the student and the issues or problems involved. In the

Learning Support example above, the tutor might demonstrate and explain the correct use of the apostrophe, then use question and answer to help the student list examples from a piece of text, and follow this by observing the student performing the task; decisions have to be made as the tutorial progresses, and much of the lesson plan may have to be expressed in rather tentative terms. In the telephone tutorial, the tutor should have made it clear what the student is expected to have done before picking up the phone, and would ensure on both sides that the encounter had been well prepared for.

Conclusion:

This might include feedback on work in progress, praise, and identification of further work that can be done. Even in cases of very specific needs the tutor might suggest follow up ideas for the student to explore and additional materials to consult and use. The next appointment will usually be confirmed at this stage.

Some of the encounters in drop-in workshops may be quite short, perhaps five minutes. Since no very detailed lesson plan can be made before they take place, it is essential for the teacher to log them afterwards. It important for the students, too, to log the session and use the information to update their own action plans.

Planning to avoid disruption

It is a fact of educational life that often in lessons and training sessions we find people whose behaviour is disruptive of the learning experiences that we devise. The Further Education Unit offers this definition of disruption: 'patterns of behaviour that significantly interrupt the learning of others' (Mansell, 1987). An important point about this description is that it focuses on the behaviour, not the student.

Often, disruptive behaviour is seen as someone's fault – the teacher or the student is to blame, or perhaps the institution is responsible. Merillie Huxley (1987) argues that this approach is unproductive, and that it better to see the situation as one where there is a *mismatch* between provision and the students' expectations and needs. So, in order to prevent disruptive behaviour in the classroom, the teacher should establish individuals' expectations and needs at the start of the course, and use this information to help make planning decisions. Needs and expectations change over time, so the tutor should monitor the situation throughout the course.

Mismatch does not always lead to disruption, of course; many learners cope well with it, but an atmosphere of openness where students are encouraged to communicate with the tutor, where there is regular evaluation of delivery and where ground rules have been established, help to prevent difficult situations from arising.

Other writers (e.g. Slavin, 1986) recommend different strategies to help prevent problems. The most important aspect of the teacher's role in this context is to communicate that learning is the key business in class time, and that class time must be used efficiently. Many classroom observation studies in schools have revealed that surprisingly little time is spent 'on task' (the time individual students actually spend actively working), and this can lead to some forms of disruptive behaviour. Slavin observes that late, disorganised starts are the most damaging example of this; early finishes can communicate that the business of learning is not being taken seriously, too. Points to plan for and to think about during planning and delivery are:

- start the lesson promptly, with an interesting engaging activity;
- make the session as varied as possible, using different teaching/learning strategies and stimuli;
- actively engage the students in learning;
- ensure that the level of tasks is appropriate for all the students – not too easy or too difficult;
- keep the momentum of the class up – avoid situations where students are left waiting for the teacher's attention for long periods;
- plan carefully for transitions from one activity to another or from one topic to another, making sure these are managed efficiently and linked together;
- stay alert to students' behaviour at all times, and intervene early if there are problems;
- use questions about progress to keep individuals focused on tasks: e.g. 'how's it going?' or non-verbal signals like eye contact;
- give praise when behaviour is right.

More serious problems may not be solved in this way, and tutors will need to take up individual cases through the tutorial system, or with the institution's counselling service.

Communication issues

Certain social classes and ethnic groups possess and use versions of English which may vary considerably from the norm of what we might call 'standard' English. The level of competence in the use of this version of the language can have great effects upon the learner's progress in any subject or discipline. 'Standard' English is the language of textbooks and the vast bulk of any other print material; it is also, by and large, the language of instruction, the language of teachers. Many students, therefore, will require some supplementary teaching in order that they can profitably gain from the subject teaching on offer. For teachers working in an area where English is not the first language of many students, it is clearly doubly important to ensure that sufficient support is available to the students to enable them to achieve the necessary standard of English. There is some learning for teachers to do here, too.

Earlier in this text, when we examined different models of the teacher, we made the point that teaching is not simply a matter of transmitting facts and information, and that communication is a complex process. We know that when learners receive information by hearing, or reading or observing, their perception of information will be influenced by what they already know, by their motivation, by their attitudes, and by cultural factors. Other communications issues which are of concern to the teacher are the distinction between verbal and non-verbal communication, and the importance of recognising the 'paralinguistics' of a situation.

Verbal communication

The way messages are interpreted is influenced by culture, and gender. Tannen (1995), in an example which has relevance to teaching, observed that there were marked differences between Japanese and American women when they corrected their children. The Japanese women expressed themselves indirectly, in ways that in the American context would mean a loss of status for the parent. The American women, in precisely the opposite way, showed their status by giving the children direct orders. Differences like these may make communication with students from different cultures difficult; the teacher can only try to be sensitive, and not to belittle students' reactions, even if they seem initially to make little sense within the teacher's frame of reference.

Gender influences the way we communicate, too. Tannen (1995) gives several examples of women and men valuing direct and indirect feedback in different ways, and there is some evidence that women receive less attention from teachers, or that the attention is of a different nature from that accorded to male students (see Chapter 9 of Ashcroft & Foreman-Peck, 1994).

Technical language can cause problems. If the teacher uses a technical term, which is unfamiliar to some or all the learners, a breakdown in communication is likely to happen. The teacher needs to explain (and spell) specialist terms; often a glossary is helpful. The folklore of technical education and training relates instances of craft apprentices writing 'Sitting Gills' at the head of their City and Guilds exam papers!

All students can benefit if the lecturer encourages their communication skills. Reece & Walker give some helpful advice.

- *speak clearly and loudly so that all can easily hear;*
- *do not read from notes; look at students when speaking and maintain eye contact;*
- *be enthusiastic about the topic;*
- *use gestures for emphasis and avoid distracting mannerisms;*
- *use visual aids to assist the spoken word but be careful that they do not become the main form of communication;*
- *encourage questions from the students.*

(Reece & Walker, 1997: 375)

Lecturers must listen carefully to what students have to say, too; communication is, after all, a two-way process.

Non-verbal communication

Teachers and students convey messages to each other non-verbally as well as verbally. These methods of communication include:

- gestures (movements of the arms and hands)

- posture and movement of the body
- proximity (how close people stand or sit when taking to each other)
- movements of the head
- eye contact
- facial expressions
- use of physical contact
- appearance, including clothing.

Many of these ways of communication convey important information about a person's mood or attitude – think about a teacher standing up straight, making eye contact with students and smiling in contrast with a teacher who is slumped, unsmiling and avoiding looking students in the eye. In order to establish a welcoming, purposeful atmosphere in the session, the teacher's non-verbal signals are important. Like other forms of communication this is also a two-way process – teachers 'read' students' non-verbal signals, too. However, teachers need to be cautious: many of these signals are culturally determined, and teachers need to bear in mind that many signals – especially gestures – can be misunderstood.

The following points are important when teaching:
- make sure the class can see you – gestures will help them understand what you are saying, but be careful not to use gestures too much, as this can distract the students' attention;
- make sure you can see them, in order to pick up their non-verbal signals;
- make sure you make eye contact with your students;
- if your words do not match your non-verbal signals, students will probably pay more attention to the signals, possibly because words are more easily faked.

Paralinguistics

The 'paralinguistic' elements of speech include intonation (the rhythmic ups and downs of speech); pauses and hesitations, speed of speaking, and so on. All of these convey information to the listener over and above the meanings of the words used. And they are particularly important if there are no visual cues to meaning, as we have noticed in our comment on the telephone tutorial above.

The teacher needs to remember:
- try not to let nervousness make you speak too quickly;
- try to vary loudness, speed and intonation to provide variety for the listener (without sounding artificial!);
- try to use tone, loudness to make the important points stand out;
- make sure that periods of exposition are relatively short: a typical concentration span when listening is 5–8 minutes;
- check that everyone can hear you – some classrooms have very poor acoustics.

All of these communications issues will contribute to decisions made as to the overall teaching strategy to select.

4.   Choosing a Teaching Strategy

In this section we will look at a number of strategies, ranging from the teacher-centred methods towards the more student-centred ones. The amount of control a teacher wishes to have will depend on the strategy chosen, as David Minton illustrates:

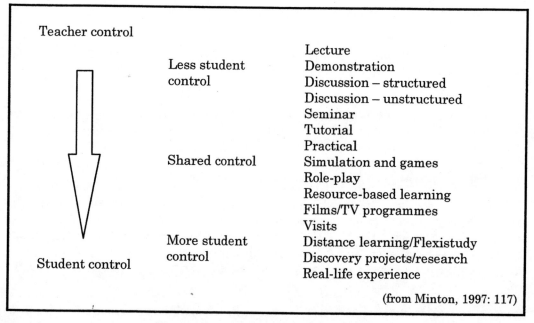

Figure 13   Control and management

However, handing over 'control' to the students does not mean an abdication of duty or that the teacher is not required to plan learning activities equally carefully; the tutor remains in a position of responsibility at all times for the students' experiences and psychological safety.

Most of the strategies described in this section are taken from those enumerated in Minton's list. They may be mainly teacher-centred, such as a lecture, or mainly student-centred, such as project work. Each teacher will need to identify strategies to suit the specific teaching context, and select those which are likely to achieve the learning outcomes and work best for the particular students.

It is most important to try to vary the strategies to maintain student interest. As a rule, student-centred, participatory activities lead to a higher level of student involvement and motivation compared to strategies that are teacher-centred and allow the learners to be less active, but it is important to remember that no approach is 'right' or 'wrong'. The teacher also needs to feel comfortable with the selected method.

Lecture

This way of teaching is sometimes called 'verbal exposition' (VE) or 'teaching by telling'. This may be used in a very formal lecture, in a lecture theatre, or as a section of a lesson in a less formal setting, such as a classroom, a workshop, a computer room or a laboratory. Often teachers use exposition in combination with the chalkboard (talk'n'chalk), or with handouts, sometimes in combination with dictation. You would use this when you wish to convey information, give instructions, provide the outline of a session or summary of a previous lesson, or give an explanation of concepts and ideas.

It is important to structure the information carefully. Many people begin with a summary of the key points and end also with a summary. You might wish to divide the lecture into sections, and use the time between each section to recap, and to make links between ideas.

You will need to provide stimulation and/or involve students actively – particularly if the exposition lasts for more than ten minutes. If you are using a handout, you may wish to pause while the students read it. Alternatively, you might provide an outline of the talk (with copies of your overheads). You might use this approach in combination with others, such as Q&A and paired work.

Remember to help students with short attention spans and poorly developed note-taking skills (we have said that most people's concentration span is 5–8 minutes). Make eye contact with the students – even in lecture theatres you can learn from students' non-verbal signals. Bear in mind that just because you have enjoyed giving a lecture, it does not mean that everyone else has enjoyed it, or has understood the content.

Some students, those with dyslexia for example, may find it particularly helpful to have printed notes, or to be able to record lectures. Deaf or hard of hearing students may find it helpful to be close to the front of the class; make sure you have attracted these students' attention when you start speaking.

Demonstration

Most teachers, not just those who teach 'practical' subjects, show students how to do things. It is vital that the teacher should describe, explain and discuss with students what is being done as well. It is important to break complex skills down into simpler sub-skills.

Often the teacher demonstrates the skill; alternatively, you might consider:

- learner-directed demonstration: teacher invites students to direct his or her operations, or to give a running commentary;
- student operation: one student carries out the task, following other students' instructions or the teacher's instructions;
- recorded demonstration; this enables the teacher (or the students working at their own pace) to play and replay the video – at full speed, half speed, or pausing if appropriate.

You might choose this when you wish to model correct behaviour, or observable skills: in the laboratory (e.g. titration), in the training restaurant (e.g. how to lay a table), at a computer (e.g. how to underline text), in a simulated workplace (e.g. how to answer the telephone) or in the classroom (e.g. how to enter items in a profit and loss account, how to punctuate, how to plan for an essay).

A teacher may be able to carry out tasks without being aware of the complexity of the skills involved. The skill needs to be analysed carefully (i.e. broken down into simple steps), and the demonstration must be short and focused on key aspects of the skill. This is why video can be so useful; it can also provide an operator's-eye view of the activity rather than an onlooker's view.

Involving the students by explaining and discussing the concepts which lie behind the skill helps the students to form principles of operation – general ideas about how they can deal with tasks like these, which help the students to transfer these skills to other, similar tasks. Maintaining eye contact with the students can be difficult during demonstrations. It is particularly important for students with hearing impairments to be able to see the tutor's face when key points are being explained.

Question and Answer (Q&A)

A question and answer session can be initiated by the teacher or by one of the students. Teachers' questions are often in writing, for example on worksheets – we will return to the design and use of these later. In this section, we will concentrate on questioning as part of the oral exchange in a classroom.

Douglas Barnes (1971) was one of the first writers to distinguish between open and closed questions. A closed question is one which has only one acceptable answer, e.g.

- What is the capital of Kenya?
- What is the atomic number of iodine?

An open question is one which has a number of acceptable answers, e.g.

- What do think about this painting?
- Why might you use a spreadsheet?

A teacher may have many different reasons for asking questions. Successful questioning depends on being clear about the purpose of the question and preparing it carefully. Many of the questions you ask will be to encourage the students to engage actively with the content of the lesson:

- to ask for facts
- to ask for descriptions
- to ask for opinions
- to ask for explanations/reasons/interpretations
- to check understanding/reveal lack of understanding
- to encourage reflection on experience
- to pose problems.

Habeshaw *et al* (1992) recommend the use of open questions during the initial phase of a lesson to help orientation. For example, 'How did you get on with the reading?' or 'How did the practical lesson go?'

Some questions may be more directly related to classroom management:

- to ask for co-operation ('Who would like to go first on this one?')
- to ask for the group's preferences (Would they prefer to work in pairs on a particular task or alone?)

Give students time to think about their answers – put the questions on the board or OHP, or on a handout. If you have asked a question orally, allow some silence while the students think, and try not to answer your own questions! It is often a good idea to target a named student to provide the answer – remember the old slogan: Pose (the question); Pause (while the students consider the answer); Pounce (on the selected student, probably someone who looks 'ready' to answer). Closed questions can discourage students who are afraid of giving the wrong answer. Encourage quieter students' participation by using open questions and allowing them to work out answers in pairs or small groups.

As in everyday life, not all questions are genuine questions. Pseudo questions, though expressed in the form of questions, are really disguised commands or instructions, e.g. 'Can we now move on to the next problem?'

Other pseudo questions appear to be open, though the teacher is, in reality, looking for a specific answer. For example, a question like 'What do you think makes people shop at Benneton?' may really be a closed question, because the teacher has a fixed response in mind ('advertising'), which is needed to move the lesson on. It is better to try to avoid this type of pretence; students find it very frustrating! Plan how you're going to ask a few key questions in every lesson, and try to vary the kinds of questions asked. Avoid using questions that are really an invitation to the student to repeat what you have just said. Try to build on a student's response to a question by inviting further comments and contributions. In a room where the students all face the front, the tutor may need to repeat student responses so that the other members of the group can hear what has been said. This is particularly important if anyone in the group has a hearing impairment. Take care not to ask too many questions as this can make a lesson seem like a cross-examination in a trial.

Large group discussion

In a discussion members of the group talk together about a topic, issue or problem. Discussions can be teacher-led or student-led; can involve the whole class or the class divided into small groups. Remember, though, that terms such as 'discussion group', 'seminar' and 'tutorial' do not have standardised meanings, and can refer to different things in different contexts.

Teachers often find it difficult to involve all the students in the group. Habeshaw *et al* (1992) offer the following advice:

Getting students to speak

Teachers often complain that they have difficulty getting students to speak in tutorials and students for their part may regard an invitation to participate as 'being picked on'. The main reason for this is that teachers and students alike seem to believe that while teachers can require students to read books, write essays and sit examinations, they don't have the right to ask them to speak. Other common reasons for students' reluctance to participate in a tutorial are that they don't know the ground rules, they are afraid of exposing themselves in public, or simply that they sense that the teacher really wants to do all the talking.

If, however, you really want your students to speak and you believe you have the right to ask them to speak and you are looking for ways of making it easier for them, you could start by discussing expectations and ground rules. Exchange views about how you would like the tutorials to be, tell them about your plans for getting them to speak (see below), and specify any ground rules. For example, students often assume that there is a ground rule that all discussion should be conducted through the chair and that they should apologise if they speak directly to another student. If you want a free ranging discussion, you will need to introduce the opposite ground rule – 'Anyone is allowed to speak to anyone' – and demonstrate your support for it by the way you behave. You could emphasise its importance by giving the students some practice straight away. You could say, 'I'm aware that because I'm a member of staff, you tend to listen more to what I say and address your remarks to me rather than to others in the group. If you do this, the discussion never really gets off the ground and we waste the benefits of being in a group. So what I'd like to suggest is that I keep silent for the next half hour and you continue the discussion. You know enough about this topic to be able to do that quite easily. I shall sit here quietly but if I think my presence is inhibiting you, I'll leave the room for half an hour. I'm going to stop speaking now'.

Students also tend to assume that the teacher is the only person who is allowed to invite people into the discussion, which is a pity because they often know more about their friends' special knowledge and interests than the teacher does. It's good to hear one student say to another, 'You know about this, don't you, Mandy? What was it you were saying yesterday?' You could encourage this by introducing a further ground rule: 'Anyone is allowed to bring another person into the discussion'.

(Habeshaw, Habeshaw & Gibbs, 1992: 63–64)

Discussions need to be summarised, recorded or presented in some way. Students can record key points for themselves at the end of the discussion, or the group leader (who may or may not be the teacher) can summarise, noting points on a flip chart or board. This is an appropriate teaching method when it is important for the students to share ideas, explore situations and solve problems. Discussions also allow the students to practise communication skills.

Structured discussions are more productive than unstructured ones. They need to be planned carefully, bearing the following points in mind. There should be carefully constructed aims and outcomes for the discussion, and the students should understand what these are. For some discussions to work well, members of the group need to be familiar with the topic, or have done some reading. The teacher should check if this is the case, and adapt the strategy if appropriate. During the discussion, the tutor may need to check that the group is keeping to the topic.

In some groups, the presence of a dominant student is an issue. The problem may be dealt with by planning the session so that more students are involved (see above). However, there may be times when more specific measures need to be taken to deal with this problem. Again Habeshaw *et al* have some useful suggestions:

Getting students to stop speaking

Highly articulate or garrulous students can be as much of a problem as quiet, reserved ones. The trouble is that such students tend either to intimidate or antagonise the other students and discourage them from joining in. The situation is often complicated by the fact that teachers will encourage such students early on because they are so relieved to have someone in the group who is willing to speak.

There are several possible ways of handling this situation:

a) Distribute the speaking time among the students by using one of the methods where everyone is expected to speak.

b) When setting up sub-groups, invite the students to identify themselves as high or low contributors and then suggest that the high contributors work together and the low contributors work together.

c) Set up a situation at the beginning of each tutorial or for half an hour during a tutorial in which nobody speaks for a second time until everyone has spoken once. You will need first to explain to the group why you are doing this: that you have noticed that some people are speaking a lot and some people a little and that you want to try to redress the balance.

d) If you have such a serious problem with an individual that none of the above suggestions work, then you will have to confront her on her own, explain how you feel about her behaviour and ask her to change it, offering your help if she needs it.

(Habeshaw, Habeshaw & Gibbs, 1992: 79)

It is important that all the students in the group including the quieter more tentative members and the ones who may try to dominate discussion are all treated respectfully by the tutor and the other members of the group. Planning strategies to ensure that the discussion is controlled and involves everyone appropriately is one way of managing this.

Another aspect of group management in face-to-face situations is the layout of the room. Ideally, for a discussion, the students should sit in a circle so that all the members of the group can see each other. This may involve changing the seating arrangements before or even during the lesson. Moving around can help to provide a signal that there is a shift from teacher-centred to student-centred learning, for example. However, the teacher should be sensitive if any student finds changing position difficult.

Remember that discussion can be difficult for hearing-impaired students – they may not know who is speaking and who to watch for lip reading. Members of the group can help by indicating with a gesture when they are speaking. Blind students can be helped if the other participants give their names when making a contribution.

Variations on the discussion method are debates – where the group is divided into two sides who take opposing views on an issue, often with a vote at the end – and 'round robins'. Here, each member of the group takes it in turn to say something about the topic. Interruptions are not allowed, so this approach encourages everyone to participate; for anxious students, it can be preceded by paired work to prepare a contribution. It is often used at the end of a lesson or course to summarise or revise.

Small group and paired work

The class is divided into small groups, triads (threes) or dyads (pairs) for discussion, writing, problem solving. This requires the active involvement of the learner: working with others can be enjoyable, and can provide support for individuals. It can offer the students a more private space to express themselves and explore views and ideas. More experienced or more able students can be encouraged to help others.

This method is appropriate when you wish to encourage more inhibited students to talk in the relative privacy of a small group or a pair. It is particularly useful to consider using small groups in contexts where the students spend much of their time working alone. Huddlestone & Unwin (1997) observe:

> Given the emphasis in FE on individualised learning, and particularly on the outcome based model as advocated by NCVQ, there is a danger that learning in colleges may become too individualised. Whilst groups of students may be together in the same space, they might all be working completely separately on different tasks... The collegiality created by group based learning can act as an important locus of support for students who lack confidence, have problems outside college or who gain extra motivation from the discipline of having to keep up with their peers.
>
> (Huddlestone & Unwin, 1997: 80)

However, groups may not necessarily offer a 'safe' space for individuals, and problems may arise from the presence of dominant members or 'star speakers'.

Some students may prefer – or are more used to – more structured forms of teaching-dominated learning, and will perceive group work as unproductive. The teacher needs to make the aims and outcomes clear, and ground rules for the group need to be observed.

The composition of groups within a class needs to be planned. Sometimes, it is appropriate to encourage friendship groups to work together; at other times the teacher may wish to vary this. The transition from large group to small group and back again needs to be managed smoothly. If any of the students are in wheelchairs or cannot move easily, this must be taken into account.

Feedback to the whole class is an important part if groupwork is used. It is important to indicate at the start of groupwork that this will happen, and to plan how it will be done and to allocate time for it on the lesson plan.

Tutorial/one-to-one

One-to-one teaching/learning takes place in a variety of contexts: training sessions in the workplace, tutorials, language training for executives, and drop-in workshops when students attend voluntarily with a variety of problems. Many teachers engage with individual students at certain points in a lesson when students are involved in projects and in solving problems: in laboratories, IT classes, numeracy workshops and in Art and Design sessions. One-to-one teaching offers an excellent opportunity to identify an individual student's strengths and weaknesses and to negotiate a study plan to suit an individual's needs.

You would choose this when providing learning or pastoral support for the student in a context which gives more privacy than is appropriate during a lesson, for example when assessing or reviewing progress, or helping a student with individual decision making such as choosing a project title.

It is most important to observe the rules of confidentiality. A private space should be organised: a quiet corner of the classroom is sometimes appropriate, at other times greater privacy will be required.

Students are very exposed in one-to-one teaching and can feel vulnerable because there is nowhere to hide lack of knowledge, and no peer support. It is therefore important that tutors help the students to feel safe. They need to be able to listen and accept students' perspectives, they should encourage openness and offer praise and encouragement. Careful time management is required, too.

'Coaching' usually occurs in one-to-one situations. The term is often used in connection with skills teaching. Mitchell defines coaching as 'the process whereby one person provides guidance for another to improve performance, through modelling and direct instruction. It is usually associated with sports, but can readily be applied to vocational and academic subjects' (Mitchell, 1997: 21).

Role-play

Role-play and simulation activities are real or imaginary situations which are simulated in the classroom.

A role-play is often chosen when people's roles in the situation, and the feelings and attitudes associated with them, are the central concern, e.g. dealing with a difficult customer in a restaurant, or managing committee work. It must be used with great care, and clear briefing, good time management and sufficient opportunity for debriefing are required. Care needs to be taken when handling sensitive issues, and the tutor must include dissociation from the role as part of the debriefing. Tutors need to remain in control, and be ready to intervene if the activity is not leading towards the intended learning.

The related strategy of simulation is chosen when factors other than people's roles in the situation are the central concern, e.g. simulations of the effect of changing interest rates on the economy. These simulations are often computer-based.

Laboratory work

In the laboratory students work on experiments and investigations. Students usually work on a practical problem (often in pairs), following a theory lesson. In Physics, they often follow a rotation system and carry out a number of different experiments over a number of weeks.

You would use this method when students need to learn through direct experience of scientific experiment and investigation. It provides active, experiential learning for science students, and provides for the integration of theory with practical application. Some of the content of science syllabuses is specifically practical, and you will find instructions such as: 'investigate by means of experiment...', 'make accurate observation and record results...'.

Safety is a central issue in laboratories, and must take precedence over all other issues. The safety of students with disabilities requires particular attention.

The practical activities of trainee chefs in a kitchen and of hairdressing students in a salon have some similarities with laboratory work; in other ways they are more like workshops.

Workshop

This can be a resource-based workshop, equipped with worksheets, materials and/or IT facilities, which will provide the opportunity for students to work on developing skills at their own pace. Alternatively, it refers to a simulated work environment, such as a kitchen or a salon.

The resource-based workshop often gives students the opportunity to work to an individualised programme of study, catching up on basic skills, practising a foreign language, learning IT skills.

The kitchen, the beauty salon, the practice office, etc. provide a controlled environment for the demonstration of professional skills, and often give the opportunity for tutors to assess the competence of the performance of students/trainees in NVQ-based schemes.

The teacher responds to students' requests for help and guidance. Students' progress needs to be monitored and checked, and the tutor needs to recognise when it is appropriate to intervene in order to offer support. It is not easy to plan and prepare for this type of session, since the tutor reacts to student problems. However, the tutor must be familiar with the work being covered, and have identified the problems which are likely to arise.

Resource-based learning

This term is sometimes used instead of 'flexible learning', and it can be used for teacher-directed or self-directed study. It is not the same as, though it forms the basis of, distance learning.

The students learn primarily from interacting with resources. These can be paper-based or computer-based, and may have been devised specially for the students by their lecturers, or bought in from outside publishers. Many institutions now have resources centres (usually part of the library) where students can go to learn in this way. Sometimes, whole courses are delivered via such resources (for example, the Open University's degrees).

This is an appropriate method of study when students need to work at their own pace, or when attendance at a specific time or in a specific place is difficult, or when this approach particularly suits the learning style of the student.

Tutorial support and guidance is vitally important, and requires special skills. This approach may not suit all learners. Those who need and enjoy peer support, feedback and encouragement may become demotivated by learning in this way, even if alternatives to face-to-face contact are provided.

Games and quizzes

Learning (or assessing) activities can be devised in the form of games and quizzes. These might be competitive or non-competitive, paper-based or computer-based.

They give an opportunity to introduce variety or a different approach to learning. These approaches are particularly useful when revising a topic or testing student learning.

Rules should be established clearly; and the serious side to the game should be explicit. Many students do not enjoy competitive games, and can feel exposed in quizzes. In these cases, chose games where psychological safety is maintained, and where every participant wins.

Brainstorming

In the first phase of this, students find solutions to a problem by shouting out as many suggestions as they can think of. These are written down without any explanation, comment or evaluation. In the second phase, the group may accept all the solutions, or work together to find the most appropriate one.

This can be a good method when you wish learners to be creative, and to involve all the members of the group.

It is important to explain the whole process carefully from the start, and to set ground rules so that suggestions are not challenged during the brainstorm. Some teachers prepare groups by having a rehearsal brainstorm first.

Resources for teaching and learning

In very few of the situations described above will the only learning resource be the teacher. More often than not there will be books, handouts, displays, pictures, videos, artefacts and so on which will be the focus of at least some of the learner's attention. Such 'learning resources' will include a wide range of materials and equipment that can be used as part of the learning experience. The learning might be about the resources themselves – for example, films in media studies, plants in horticulture, machinery in engineering, computers in IT – though the resources are just as likely to be there to stimulate the students or help learning in virtually any learning situation. The information is often presented in the form of printed or projected text, images and diagrams, but resources might include sounds, real objects, and even scents.

Selecting the resources to be used as part of a student's learning experience is therefore an important part of the lesson planning stage, and time may have to be allowed for the preparation of materials. The choice is wide, as learning resources (we may still refer to them as 'teaching/learning aids') can include:

- printed materials – handouts, task sheets, etc.
- photographs and slides
- posters
- models
- boards – chalk board, white board, or magnetic board
- flip charts
- overhead transparencies (also known as OHTs)
- audio tapes and compact discs
- tape-slide sequences (synchronised audio tapes and slides)
- video tapes and film
- laboratory equipment
- real objects (sometimes referred to as 'realia')
- computer-based resources – databases, computer conferencing, information from websites, etc.

An important planning decision for teachers is whether to use (or adapt) existing material or to design and produce their own. Producing materials is very time consuming, but the result can be more appropriate to particular students' needs. Whether of your own design or taken from other sources, materials should be evaluated at the planning stage.

General questions to use when evaluating resources:

- are the materials appropriate to the learning outcomes, in terms of content and treatment?

- are they suitable in terms of the characteristics of the students, that is, their age, experience, motivation, etc?

- are they clear and attractive and consistent with a professional approach to teaching?

- are they reasonably cost effective?

- are they suitable for the way they will be used? (Will the teacher introduce and mediate the resources, or will students use them working independently?)

- are they free from any sexist, racist or homophobic language or images? It is important to avoid stereotypes; for example don't reinforce stereotypes by showing women secretaries and male managers. Choose names in case studies that reflect life in a multi-ethnic society, even if this variety is not represented in your teaching group (don't stick to names like Smith and Jones in examples). It is particularly important to be careful with jokes and with drawings that are intended to be humorous – what is amusing to one person may offend another. (Appendix B gives guidelines on writing to avoid sexist language.)

Considerations of particular media

Printed materials – handouts, task sheets, etc.

In planning, check that the handout is not overloaded with information – a cluttered handout filled with small type is less likely to engage the students' attention. All textual material should be produced using a word processor; it may help to lay text out in columns, like newspapers, or in blocks. Text and images should be clear, and the print should be big enough for any student with visual impairment to read easily. The language used should be clear, and suitable for the reading abilities and language competences of the learners.

Handouts can be complete notes and texts, though the learners may use them for more active learning if they contain questions, tasks or sections that require completion during the session. Some tutors distribute outlines of formal lectures on handouts – often a copy of other visual aids being used. Another approach to consider is the incomplete or 'gapped' handouts. These should be used with caution: adult students sometimes dislike these, and they are less useful for a student who has missed a session.

White boards

A great advantage of the board, whether white or black, is that it can be used in unpredictable situations, for example when the tutor is responding to needs that become apparent during class time, or to note down key points from student feedback after group work. The teacher may realise during discussion that the group is unfamiliar with a technical term, and write it on the board so that the students will see it (this helps them remember) and will know how to spell it. It is useful in more planned situations, too: many tutors use the whiteboard for putting up an outline lesson plan at the start of the session, and if the board is wide enough, one half can be used for this and the other half used for the notes and jottings. Boards are less suitable for diagrams and maps: it takes too long for the tutor to draw them, and few tutors have the required artistic skills. A prepared chart or OHT (see below) is better for these.

All the students in the group must be able to read what is presented on the board (visually-impaired students may be disadvantaged if the lecturer relies heavily on information written on the board, without talking through the points carefully). It is important to use a clear writing or print style, colour pens or chalks for impact, and to leave reasonable spaces between sections of text. As with handouts, an overloaded board is less attractive for the learner. When planning board work, think about what information to put on the board and how to lay it out, and consider dividing the board into different sections as suggested above if it is big enough.

Many tutors need to practise writing on the board so that information can be presented clearly and attractively. Board work requires losing eye contact with the class, and teachers should try to not turn away from the group for too long a period. For some activities (such as feedback to the whole class after small group work) it is appropriate to ask group members to write on the board, but the tutor needs to be sensitive to the exposure that this brings to the student. Some dyslexic tutors ask the students to do this for them.

And always, but always, clean the board before you leave the room.

Flipcharts

These can be used like the board for noting student responses, and they are a good medium for students to record the product of groupwork that can be displayed and read by the whole class. They can be prepared in advance for presenting information. As with boards, colour and size of text for headings add to the impact, and overloading should be avoided.

Overhead transparencies (OHTs)

These are extremely versatile transparent sheets (or less commonly rolls) of acetate, placed on an overhead projector (OHP). They can be used in the ways described above for the board, and have the advantage that the teacher does not have to turn away from the class. The greatest advantage of OHTs, however, is that they can be prepared in advance – by hand, from photocopies or by using Information Technology. They are suitable for both text and images. If you have access to word-processing or a specialised package such as Microsoft PowerPoint, it is possible to produce scaled down versions of OHTs for distribution as handouts to students.

Transparencies, like other resources, should not be overloaded with information. There should be a maximum of 8 lines of text on a transparency. Lettering should not be smaller than 7 mm (18 point); headings should be 32 point or 28 point.

There are a number of different ways of presenting OHTs. Apart from showing the whole transparency at once, the lecturer can focus attention to a particular point by covering up the rest of the information. This may be done by placing paper on the transparency and sliding it off to reveal successive lines of information, or placing cards, coins or 'post its' on sections of the transparency and removing them at appropriate points in the lecture. Complex diagrams can be built up by placing one transparency on top of another in overlays. If the students need the diagrams on the OHTs as part of their notes, it is better to provide a copy of the diagrams for them as a handout, rather than spend class time unproductively while they copy them down.

And remember that if you wish to point to anything on the transparency, use a pencil rather than your finger, and don't walk over to stand by the screen.

Computer-based resources

The most commonly used application of Information Technology by teachers is the production of resources like handouts and OHTs. If there is access to appropriate equipment, PowerPoint displays can be projected using an OHP and a lap top personal computer, or a large computer screen. And, of course, many learners learn how to use IT as part of their studies, often through learning how to use industry standard applications like word processing and spreadsheets.

However, an important and growing use of IT is to support learning in specific curriculum areas. Some of these use the applications referred to above: spreadsheets can be used in mathematics, engineering, catering, etc. Sometimes this can be a straightforward use of the applications program: maths students use spreadsheets to present graphs and pie-charts, catering students for budgeting, history students use databases. These applications can be used in different ways: spreadsheets for mathematical modelling, word processing for editing and producing broadsheets in communications classes.

Students are often motivated by gaining access to the resources provided by using CD ROMs and to constantly updated information on the Internet. CD ROMs can be evaluated before use in ways similar to that for printed materials, but it is harder for a tutor to check materials from the Internet: and screening for offensive resources (e.g. racist, sexist and homophobic material) remains an issue.

Other ways of using technology provide support for learning: computer conferencing or email to communicate with peers and tutors, and interactive learning packages on CD ROM and on the World Wide Web.

Other resources

Extracts from films and television programmes, real objects, and paintings should be evaluated in the same way as paper-based resources. Films and television programmes should be used in conjunction with tasks to encourage the learners to engage actively with the materials. Photography and video can be used to record the progress and the achievement of students.

A final reminder: all materials are subject to the laws of copyright, and if you photocopy or otherwise reproduce such materials you must check that they are free from copyright or that you have permission to use them.

5.   Lesson Appraisal and Evaluation

Evaluation, or lesson appraisal, is part of the cyclical, reflective process that we looked at earlier (see Figure 3 on page 7). It refers to the process of checking how effective teaching or the provision for learning has been; this should not be confused with assessment, which refers to the measurement of student achievement, and is considered in detail in Sections 6 to 10 of this text.

Evaluation, therefore, provides teachers with information which will help them to improve the structuring and delivery of a topic in the future; it should also give the opportunity for a wider reflection on more general skills and activities. At the programme level, course and curriculum evaluation are important components of an institution's quality assurance strategy.

The process of evaluating a training or teaching session should begin at the planning stage, and lesson plans should include strategies for gathering information about the students' experience. The process of assessment of learning will provide some of this feedback for the tutor, but other strategies for evaluation should be considered. These will be discussed in this section.

Methods of lesson evaluation

Self-evaluation
A popular way to do this is for the tutor to complete a check list or note down answers to a series of prompt questions. There are many published examples of check lists and questions, (see, for example, Brown *et al.* 1993). Many of these have been designed to be used as observation instruments, and need to be adapted for self-evaluation. It is important for the teacher to see these as tools which can be altered to suit different groups and contexts. Teachers often find it useful to choose to focus on specific aspects of a particular session.

Case study

Javita teaches a weekly evening class, 'An Introduction to Assertiveness' in an Adult Education Centre. Over the past few weeks, she has been concerned about her time management during the session. Toward the middle of the session, she organises small group work, then a plenary session, where groups report back to the whole class. This should be followed by her planned closing section, where she summarises the evening's work, takes questions and previews the following week's work. However, there is never enough time for the final section, and it is always rushed.

Javita therefore decides to monitor her timing closely, and record her timing carefully the following week. She also distributes a short questionnaire, which asks her class members to comment on which section of the evening they have found most useful.

Continued...

> This combination of self-evaluation and feedback from the group reveals that she has spent longer than she planned on the plenary, and that the students find this section of the session 'slow'.
>
> Javita decides to investigate other methods of gathering feedback after group work which will allow her to debrief the group work more speedily and will provide a more varied and stimulating experience for the group.

Evaluation should be done as soon as possible after the class, when it is easier to recall what has happened.

Some questions for self-evaluation might be:

Did I achieve my aims and learning outcomes?

- Did you have too many or too few intended outcomes?
- Had you pinned them down exactly enough so that you were confident of what you were doing and why you were doing it?
- Were the outcomes appropriate to the needs and levels of the class?
- If not, how do you need to alter them?

Were my teaching strategies suitable?

- Did any of your planned activities fail to work effectively?
- If so, what were the reasons?
- Did you have enough variety in order to keep students interested and challenged?
- Did you have so much variety that students were becoming confused and lost?

Was my choice of aids and resources appropriate?

- Did your resources help or hinder?
- Did any of them not work as well as you had hoped?
- If so, what can you do to improve matters next time?
- Were there any occasions when you felt you needed an aid or resource but you hadn't got one?

How successful were my assessment techniques?

- If you were mainly relying on oral questions, did the students seem to understand your questions and give the kind of replies you had hoped for?
- If not, what can you do about it?
- If you were using written assessment, was the task you set an appropriate one to let the students show what they had learnt?
- Similarly, was any demonstration of a skill that you asked of them an appropriate one?

How successful was my timing?

- Did you cover as much as you had expected when you planned the lesson?
- Were the timings of the various phases of the lesson roughly accurate?
- Did some activities or sections take a longer or shorter time than you had anticipated? Why was this?
- Did you feel under pressure towards the end of the lesson to hurry in order to get through what you had planned?
- Did this hurrying adversely affect your teaching?
- What can you do to make sure that you aren't trying to put a quart of teaching in to a pint-pot of time?

What were my relationships with the class like?

- How did you get on with the students?
- Did you have any class management/discipline problems?
- Did any particular students give you special trouble or indeed support?
- Were the students interested, involved and responsive?

Did I divert from the plan?

- If yes, what caused the diversion?
- Were your timings a bit wrong?
- Did an activity fail to work very well?
- Did some students refuse to do something?

Are there any modifications I ought to make for next time?

- What benefits would follow from these modifications?
- Are they general changes to your teaching or specific to this particular class or topic?

Collecting feedback from learners

A number of approaches are used to collect information from students, including questionnaires (devised by the teacher or by the learners), interviews, discussions led by the teacher, the students or by a third party. It is crucial to remember that some students may fear that negative feedback will affect their assessment grades. This concern, however unfounded, may prevent students from being completely open, particularly in face-to-face situations, and tutors may wish to select evaluation methods which preserve students' anonymity.

Two of the more frequently used methods of evaluation are questionnaires and discussions. Institutions or clients frequently require formal questionnaires as part of their monitoring procedures. More often than not these are used at the end of a course when it is too late to alter anything for that particular cohort of students.

Trainers and teachers often design their own less formal versions to provide feedback that can be used to help adjust planned sessions to meet a particular group's needs.

Questionnaires might contain closed questions about knowledge or skills acquired:

Do you feel confident now about drawing straight line graphs? Yes/No

or more open invitations like:

What did you find most useful about this evening's session?

Busy teachers may wish to design something quickly. You might consider putting questions on an OHT, and asking students to write down their responses. This enables the teacher to explain any unclear question on the OHT, and still preserves anonymity.

Discussions need to be organised in a fairly structured way. A popular approach is to use the *Nominal Group Technique*. Lecturers may organise this themselves, or they might ask a colleague or the students to run the session.

Nominal group technique

Nominal Group Technique (NGT)[1] is a technique for generating ideas in groups and reflecting on them. It is similar to brainstorming in that it initially involves recording ideas without evaluating them, but it is more highly structured and specifically addresses itself to subsequent action.

NGT is particularly useful when your starting point in a discussion is the feelings and experiences of the group as, for example, the reactions of a group of students to a course. The technique brings out these initial unanalysed reactions and then provides a framework for organising and analysing them. It has much more chance of success than the unstructured discussion which starts with the question, 'Well, what did you think of the course this year, then?'

An NGT meeting normally involves eight stages:
1. Asking the question
2. Writing individual responses
3. Listing the responses
4. Clarifying the responses
5. Evaluating and ranking the responses
6. Discussion
7. Plenary
8. Planning ahead.

1) Asking the question

The students are presented with a question. This can be fairly general (e.g. 'What changes need to be made to this course?') or specific (e.g. 'What difficulties have you experienced in the organic chemistry practicals?') or personal (e.g. 'How do you feel you have developed as a person on the course so far?').

Continued...

---

2) Writing individual responses

Individuals are asked to write down their own responses to the set question, and then to rank them in order of importance. About ten minutes is allowed for this. Announce how much time is to be allowed so that students can pace themselves and work at an appropriate level of detail. Discussion is not permitted. Responses which seem trivial should not be omitted as the intention is to generate as much material as possible; analysis will take place later.

3) Listing the responses

Participants form groups of 8–10 people. Each group needs a neutral 'leader' whose role will be to co-ordinate the work of the group; this role could be performed by an 'honest broker'. Groups pool their responses to form a composite list. The leader writes the list on a board or flipchart. At this stage the items are not commented upon, criticised or edited in any way. Individuals may be influenced by other people's contributions to make additional suggestions of their own, but this should not develop into a discussion. The aim is to draw up as large a list as possible, involving all members of the group. This may take up to three-quarters of an hour.

4) Clarifying the responses

In stage 3 the responses were not explained. In stage 4 the leader takes the group through the listed responses making sure that everyone understands what they all mean. Again no discussion or criticism of the items is permitted.

5) Evaluating and ranking the responses

The purpose at this stage is to rank the items on the list. A voting system can be used. Criteria such as urgency, interest, personal concern and so on should be agreed and each item rated on a 1–5 scale according to each of the criteria (1 = least urgent, 5 = most urgent). Students can be limited to five votes altogether, to speed the process. Adding up the ratings for each item will give a crude indication of the group's perception of the list. It is intended that evaluation through discussion does not take place until this overall picture emerges.

6) Discussion

Now that the students in the group can see which responses are generally considered important, more open discussion can take place. Useful questions to move along such a discussion include 'What strikes you as interesting?' or 'What surprises you by its omission?'.

7) Plenary

At this stage the separate groups come together and the ranked lists of responses are pooled. The top ten from each group, for example, can be put together. Overlapping items can be combined or more carefully discriminated and a second voting procedure operated. The outcome is an overall ranking of the key responses so that it is quite clear what the important issues are.

Continued...

---

8) Planning ahead

Students can also be encouraged to discuss possible changes in the course and in teaching, once the key issues are clear.

(This item was written with the help of Mike O'Neill, Trent Polytechnic)

[1]Delbecq AL, Van de Ven AH & Gustafson DH. *Group techniques for program planning: a guide to Nominal and Delphi Processes,* Scott, Foresman 1975

(Gibbs, Habeshaw & Habeshaw, 1988b: 77–79)

Information collected from

- the measurement of student achievement (assessment),
- the teacher's own evaluation, and
- feedback from the students

all go to help the manager of learning to provide learning experiences that are effective.

Conclusion

It is important to remember that there are a number of factors to be taken into account in the planning of individual lessons, or a series of lessons.

The demands of the syllabus may be the starting point, but other issues are vital as well. Establishing and meeting the needs of the learners, catering for the mix of students in the group, providing a variety of learning experiences, involving students in active learning, communicating clearly, assessing learning, and evaluating in order to improve delivery, are all important. And perhaps most important of all is: establishing a productive climate in the classroom where the contributions of all the group are welcomed and encouraged. The job of teachers is to help learners to learn, and this is the central concern of planning and delivering teaching.

The level of student achievement will reveal whether or not the students or trainees have actually learned what we intended them to learn, and we turn to matters of assessment next.

Part Four – Assessment of Learning

Assessment is a major concern for those who learn, those who teach and those who are responsible for developing courses or training programmes.

- 'How will I be assessed?'; 'Are there exams?'; 'What do I have to do to pass?' are some of the questions students ask before they even start.

- 'How well are my students getting on?', 'Can my trainees really understand the subject and demonstrate the skills?' we ask ourselves as teachers.

- 'How can we be sure that the learners are achieving what the course sets out to do?' ask the programme leaders and curriculum developers.

We are all involved in making judgements about attainment or performance at some time in our professional and personal lives – either as an assessor or as the person who is assessed. Employers, colleagues and clients assess how we do our work; friends, family and magistrates may assess our behaviour; doctors assess our health and teachers assess our learning. As Rowntree (1987: xii) notes:

> ... we spend our lives assessing others, trying to know them and explain them to ourselves – and often influencing them by our consequent decisions. And even in death we cannot escape the assessors – obituary writers for the famous; just family, workmates and friends for the rest of us.

Assessment plays an important part in the teaching and learning process at all levels in education. Rowntree (1987: 1) suggests that:

> If we wish to discover the truth about an educational system, we must look into its assessment procedures. What student qualities and achievements are actively valued and rewarded by the system? How are its purposes and intentions realized? To what extent are the hopes and ideals, aims and objectives professed by the system ever truly perceived, valued and striven for by those who make their way within it? The answers to such questions are to be found in what the system requires students to **do** in order to survive and prosper. The spirit and style of student assessment defines the de facto curriculum.

There have been considerable changes in the purpose and practice of assessment over the last few decades. Huddleston & Unwin (1997: 111) note that:

> Assessment is now not so much something which is 'done unto' students but which often involves negotiations with students and sometimes with employers as well.

So in this Part we shall attempt to answer the following questions:

- What is the purpose of assessing learners?
- What is it that we assess?
- What types of assessment methods do we use?
- Who assesses learners?
- What can we do to try to ensure that assessment is fair?
- How do we go about assessing?

6.   Basic Issues

We will first discuss why assessment is important, and try to put it into a social, educational and political context. We will then go on to define what we mean by assessment.

The context

Student learning is very often assessment-driven. There is much research evidence that most learners tend to work harder for those aspects of a programme which are being assessed. This means that assessment can determine, to a certain extent, what students learn. However, assessment should be an integral part of the teaching and learning process. It should not be the main focus for learning; nor should it be just an afterthought or simply a test. Assessment provides learners and teachers with feedback and this feedback can be used to improve learning. Assessment is basic to learning and assessment methods should be integrated into a programme of study or training course when it is designed – as reflected in Figure 14 – rather than 'bolted on'.

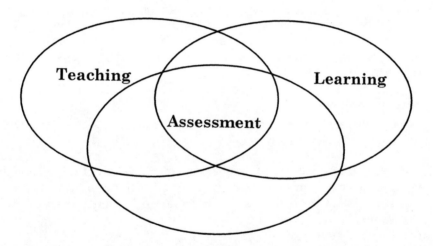

Figure 14   Assessment is an integral part of teaching and learning

(Brown & Knight, 1994: 46)

For this reason, teachers and trainers have always been aware of the importance of assessment. In recent years, however, assessment has also become a political issue. Increasingly, teachers are being required to demonstrate that students have profited from their learning. Organisations involved in teaching or training are expected to prove their 'success' with groups of learners. It is part of a changing culture, particularly since the early 1990s, which has placed an emphasis both on accountability and on a market model of education and training. Many organisations involved in training have externally set targets and, in some cases, funding is linked to the extent to which those externally set targets are met. League tables, which rank examination achievements, are published in the press. They are used, if appropriate, in organisations' promotional materials. They are also used as evidence to counter or to support arguments about education and educational standards.

For state-funded provision, there has been growing pressure to demonstrate the value of a seemingly large financial investment, to improve 'results', to meet given targets and to raise standards. For private training providers, of course, good achievement and success rates are necessary for commercial survival.

Over the years there have been trends in assessment. Perhaps the most significant recent shift has been towards an emphasis on demonstrating and assessing *competence*, often within the workplace, resulting from the introduction of new types of vocational qualifications in the late 1980s. There has also been a move towards assessing students' transferable, personal skills as well as the content of what they are studying.

Changes in assessment methods can be controversial. The contribution of continuous assessment towards final grades, for example, remains an issue for debate. It becomes topical each year when school, college or university exam results are announced. If results are higher than in the previous year, some will argue that standards must have gone down. They may conclude that the tasks, or the method of assessment, must be less rigorous. Others will argue that teaching has improved and that standards are rising in the same way as in sport, where people are now routinely achieving standards that seemed out of reach a decade ago. These issues will be explored further in later sections.

The meaning of assessment

Assessment can be described most simply as a set of devices – or tools – which are employed to measure learner achievement.

We need to be clear that 'assessment' is not the same as 'evaluation', although some authors use these two words interchangeably. We have taken evaluation to represent a broader concept than assessment. As we have seen in Section 5, teachers will often evaluate a session they teach, after the event. This will involve asking themselves questions such as: 'How did it go?', 'What could I do better next time?'

Teachers also evaluate whole courses or programmes. Often, learners as well as teachers are involved in evaluations. Students may, for example, be asked to complete questionnaires, or to participate in committee or team meetings. An evaluation of a particular training programme usually results in minor changes which are then implemented in time for the next intake of students. But an evaluation often begins by examining students' achievements. If these achievements are not satisfactory then the evaluation may result in changes being made to assessment strategies, to the teaching methods or even to the curriculum content itself.

We shall follow the practice of most educational writers and distinguish between the two terms. 'Assessment', then, is taken to refer to the tools used to measure learner achievement.

Assessment, as Rowntree (1987: 4) suggests:

> ... *can be thought of as occurring whenever one person, in some kind of interaction, direct or indirect, with another, is conscious of obtaining and interpreting information about the knowledge and understanding, or abilities and attitudes, of that other person... In education we are mainly conscious of this 'encounter' in the shape of teachers finding out about their students.*

Assessment has been further defined as:

> *a systematic basis for making inferences about the learning and development of students ... the process of defining, selecting, designing, collecting, analyzing, interpreting and using information to increase students' learning and development.*

(Erwin, 1992: 15, quoted in Brown & Knight, 1994: 12)

7.   Purposes of Assessment

Assessment is intended primarily to benefit the learner. However, many people, in addition to the learner, have an interest or a 'stake' in the outcome of someone else's learning. These stakeholders may include, for example, potential learners, working colleagues, mentors, tutors, sponsors, institutional managers, 'competing' institutions, employers and funding bodies.

Why do we need to assess?

Assessment is used for a number of purposes, among them to:

- measure the relationship between the teachers' aims and the students' output
- test the progress of students
- diagnose particular weaknesses or highlight strengths
- provide feedback to learners, leading to future improvement
- provide feedback to teachers and trainers
- provide feedback to other stakeholders, as described above
- select students for courses of study or employment
- predict future achievement
- estimate learners' current skills
- form part of a student's profile of abilities
- contribute to some publicly recognised accreditation system
- recognise prior achievement and experience and possibly to lead to credit accumulation and transfer
- demonstrate to students that they have attained some goal or acquired some skill
- motivate the learner.

In order to meet these differing needs, assessment usually has to take different forms, be undertaken at varying times and have its results communicated in various ways. Learners may require feedback early on in a course, for example, to know how well they are doing and to identify any current or potential problems. This type of assessment is known as *formative*.

An employer, on the other hand, may wish to know what a trainee can actually do at the end of a training programme. Students, too, will want this kind of *summative* verdict on completing a course of study. Before enrolling on a course, tutors may wish to identify any weaknesses students have and so they may wish to give learners a *diagnostic test*.

Formative assessment

This type of assessment is used to monitor learning progress during a course or period of training. Its prime purpose is to provide feedback to students and to the tutor so that achievement or performance can be improved. For teachers and trainers, formative assessment also provides information about how successful they have been in enabling students to learn. Usually, it confirms what the teacher already knows. Occasionally, however, it may indicate the need to change teaching strategies, for example, to provide tasks at different levels for specific individuals or to spend more time with the whole group recapping and consolidating earlier learning.

Much formative assessment is informal, that is, it is based on the tutor's observations of what is happening in the classroom or workshop; but more formal tests of various sorts are also used. Many of these are devised by teachers or trainers in the normal course of their work, although in some competence-based programmes such monitoring devices are specifically designed by the validating body to check on the ongoing achievements of students.

For the trainee or student, formative assessment provides reinforcement or a metaphorical 'pat on the back'. It may also identify specific problems, errors or weaknesses to which the student needs to pay attention.

A key aspect of continuing formative assessment is that it provides a basis for discussion between tutor and learner. Assessment is the aspect of learning or training which is most likely to cause concern for those being assessed. It is important, therefore, that students are fully aware of what is involved, what is expected and how to prepare.

Teachers need to allocate time to discuss grades and performance with students. It is important for this dialogue to take place as assessment without communication is of limited value. This communication is often of an informal nature in the class, workshop or workplace, but it can also take place effectively during scheduled one-to-one tutorial sessions, by letter, over the telephone, via email or electronic or video conferencing.

Formative assessment can provide insights for the tutor into what material needs covering again and can therefore mark the starting point for the next session. The techniques most commonly used for formative assessment typically include oral questioning in class, short answer written tests, essay or assignment tests and assessments of ongoing practical activities undertaken in workshops and classrooms.

Summative assessment

As the name implies, this type of process comes at the end – or summing up – of a programme, course, module or unit. It is typically designed to assess the extent to which learning has been achieved, the quality of students' work and, in some cases, to assign course grades and final certification.

The techniques used for summative assessments are various but may include the following:

- examinations produced by examining bodies

- projects
- teacher-produced achievement tests
- skills/competency assessment
- inspection of diaries, laboratory note-books and work experience reports
- observations of products, portfolios and craft products.

These methods of assessment, amongst others, are discussed more fully in Section 10.

Diagnostic assessment

Diagnostic assessments are used to determine the presence or absence of necessary skills or knowledge. They may also determine the underlying causes of repeated learning difficulties. A diagnostic test may highlight, for example, that a student on a vocational course is struggling with his or her studies because of a lack of adequate numeracy skills. Once identified, appropriate support can be given to this learner.

The differences between formative, summative and diagnostic assessment are not always clear cut. If coursework contributes to a final grade, for example, it becomes part of the summative assessment. Any formative assessment of that coursework, therefore, does not necessarily provide the student with the opportunity to improve.

Formative and summative assessment can also be used for diagnostic purposes. Diagnostic assessment may be lost in some cases if composite or aggregate grades mean that students are unable to identify their particular strengths or weaknesses.

Product and process

When thinking about assessment, we have a tendency to focus solely on the product outcomes of the students' learning. We think, for example, about the artefacts learners may produce in studios, kitchens or workshops; written work in the form of assignments, projects or exam answers; output from a computer printer or screen; or oral answers to questions given in a classroom or at the workplace.

As we have already noted, there has been a trend towards formally assessing students' transferable, personal skills as well as the content of what they are studying. Sometimes we have educational outcomes which require the assessment of processes – such as motivation, work habits and relationships with other people.

The method which is most appropriate in many cases for this type of assessment is observation by teachers, who recognise many different sorts of characteristics of their students during the times that they are with them. We note the students who are effective in the use of their time and we note those who are persistent and hardworking. In discussion sessions we might observe that some are not only more willing than others to speak but that they seem more capable of framing their thoughts cogently. We may also note learners' reactions to praise and criticism as well as their sensitivity or bigotry.

Product and process can be so closely intertwined sometimes that it may be difficult to identify precisely which is being assessed. This may be the case, for example, when assessing a presentation by students or a group project.

Competence

We mentioned earlier the increasing emphasis on the measurement of competence. Most vocational qualifications have been designed as – or converted into – NVQs (National Vocational Qualifications), following the establishment in 1986 of the National Council for Vocational Qualifications (NCVQ), since incorporated into the Qualifications and Curriculum Authority (QCA).

The analogy of the practical driving test, with which most people are familiar, is often used to illustrate this competence-based approach. As long as you are 17 years old, there are few restrictions in taking the driving test. You can take it at any time of the year. You can be taught by friends or relatives or you can seek, and pay for, specialist training from a range of providers. You may wish to take the test without having had any training if you feel you are competent and ready to be assessed. If you do not pass the test, you can keep trying until you do. You are not competing with anyone else.

Like the NVQ assessor, the driving test examiner may not be concerned about how, when, where and for how long you had prepared for the test. He or she is only interested in assessing competence, although we might hold that there is an additional 'knowledge-based' component in the form of a written test on the Highway Code. Assessment is independent of mode of learning. Again, like the NVQ assessor, the examiner uses national standards to assess your performance.

The competence-based model, therefore, looks at what candidates can *do*. The assessment should be under conditions which are as closely related to working conditions as possible – ideally, in the workplace itself. Candidates are either competent or 'not yet competent' in relation to specific learning outcomes.

The qualifications are written in the form of competences which are related to those skills likely to be found in daily use in industry and commerce. Thus, competences should represent national practices. These competences are endorsed by those responsible for employment in the industry. Having established national levels of competence (see below), NCVQ invited industry to form 'Industry Lead Bodies' (now 'National Training Organisations'), which represented the employers in these occupational areas. Competences are hierarchically structured in levels and relate to higher and higher levels of performance.

- Level 1 – recognises competence in a range of work activities which are primarily routine and predictable or which provide a broad foundation.

- Level 2 – recognises competence in a broader and more demanding range of work activities involving greater responsibility.

- Level 3 – recognises competence in skilled areas that involve performance of a broad range of work activities including many that are complex and non-routine. Supervisory competence may be a requirement at this level.

- Level 4 – recognises competence in the performance of complex, technical and professional work activities, including supervision or management.

- Level 5 – 'higher level' – recognises competence in the pursuit of a senior occupation or profession (as an employee or as a self-employed person) including the ability to apply a significant range of fundamental principles and techniques to diagnosis, planning and problem solving. Extensive knowledge and understanding will be required to underpin competence at this level, together with capability in management and supervision for executive and some professional fields.

While there are considerable advantages to the competence approach, there are also many concerns about this model of assessment. One of the most serious is the debate about *degrees* of competence. Some would argue that simply 'can do' is not enough and that there is no incentive in this model to excel. Think about the people who might undertake work for you, your family or your friends – hairdressers, dentists, builders or car mechanics – and the expectations you have of their competence. If you need to call out a plumber in an emergency, you would probably want a *very good* plumber, not one who once demonstrated competence according to what might be considered as minimum standards. In identifying what he calls 'shades of competence', Race (1993) highlights the difficulties in deciding exactly what we mean by competence (see Figure 15).

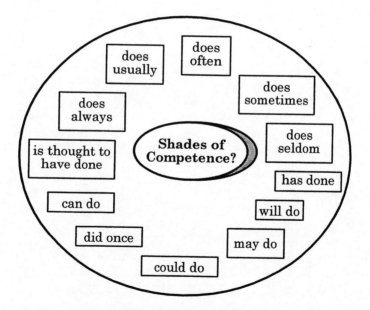

Figure 15 Shades of competence

(Race, 1993: 42)

Race then goes on to suggest some descriptors, which demonstrate the difficulties in assessing competence (see Figure 16).

Figure 16 Some competence descriptors

(Race, 1993: 43)

In most competence-based programmes, learners are assessed according to prescribed *performance criteria* as written by the Lead Bodies, or National Training Organisations (NTOs) as they are now known.

We shall be looking at examples of performance criteria in the next section.

8.   Types of Assessment

We need now to explore more carefully what we mean by 'criteria' and introduce two important terms in relation to types of assessment – *norm-referenced* and *criterion-referenced*. We will start with a hypothetical example, based on an idea by Brown & Pendlebury (1992), to demonstrate the meaning of these terms.

A caveman says to his daughter 'Now go out and kill your first bear'. This task is an example of criterion-referenced assessment. Criteria provide a list of things that a learner should be able to do in order to complete a course of study successfully. In this example, there is only one criterion – to kill a bear. This criterion has to be met in order to succeed and the learner will either pass or fail. If the task had been changed to 'Go out and kill as many bears as you can' and it had been given to all the children in the locality, then the test would have been a norm-referenced task which put candidates in rank order based on their scores.

Let us look at the purpose of this exercise. If this task had been used to measure the extent of learning at the end of a hunting training course it would have been summative. If, on the other hand, it had been used during the training in order to provide feedback to the children on how well their hunting skills were developing, it could be described as formative.

Norm-referenced assessment

Norm-referenced assessment compares one person's performance with that of everyone else being assessed, either in the present or over a period of time. It places students in rank order or on a *normal distribution curve*. Figure 17 over the page shows a typical normal distribution curve with 90% of students passing, 10% of them with merits and the top 10% with distinctions. The lowest 10% have failed. Although these percentages may remain the same from year to year, the cut-off point for a fail, merit or distinction will change depending on the knowledge and skills of the learners undertaking the particular assessment. So a pass-mark one year may lead to failure the next.

If everyone is coached for the exam, for example, the standard and quality of work may go up considerably for all students, and improved grades may show this. However, the lowest 10% of students will probably continue to fail.

There must be a good spread of marks and the questions must discriminate well between students. If all students get marks of 90%–100% or all get marks below 10% the norm-referencing system breaks down because it cannot then be used effectively to rank-order performance. Norm-referenced assessment determines a level at which someone is deemed to have been successful. Even within a classroom setting a tutor may, for example, describe a student's performance as 'being within the top 5%' of her class. Had that student been in the group in the previous year, she may not have been in the top 5%.

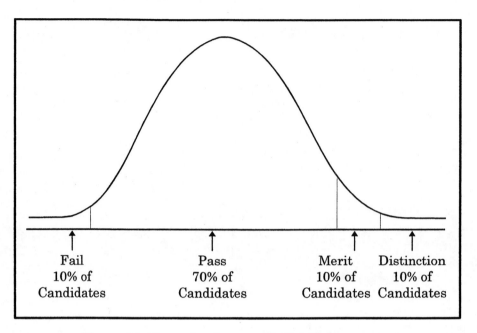

Figure 17 Example of a normal distribution curve

Although norm-referencing is still commonly used in formal – especially nationwide – assessments, it receives much criticism. It may demonstrate people's relative standing but it says little, if anything, about what they can actually do. It also makes many of those involved in the process feel like failures. Some of you – or your friends and relatives – may have experienced this type of assessment in the past. You may, for example, remember the 11+ exam or General Certificate of Education (GCE) 'O' levels, the precursor to GCSEs.

Norm-referenced tests are an essential component of any system which is based on selection, and is likely to be favoured by those who believe that competition with others is an essential component of the educational process.

Criterion-referenced assessment

Criterion-referenced assessment, on the other hand, sets out a list of things that a learner has to be able to do to demonstrate *mastery*. If these things can be done to the required level, then the learner succeeds, regardless of how many other students can or cannot achieve them.

Instead of comparing students with each other, a candidate's performance is assessed against some independent, free-standing definition of what should be achieved. In theory, all learners in a group could succeed or all could fail. To pass, you need simply to meet all the criteria. The practical driving test is criterion-referenced.

Let us look at an example of the use of such criteria. Students on a course leading to a teaching qualification for the PCET sector are likely to be asked to plan a teaching session, teach it and evaluate it, and design an overall scheme of work. The criteria for assessment may look something like this:

The work must show:
a) a professional approach to the preparation and planning of teaching
b) coherence and appropriate organisation in the scheme of work
c) competence in the delivery of the session
d) evidence of the ability to reflect on own performance and to respond positively to constructive feedback.

Figure 18 Example of assessment criteria

Assessment based on the public statement of performance criteria has been promoted by policy makers and qualification designers over the last few decades. The Certificate of Secondary Education (CSE), introduced in the early 1980s, was intended to be criterion-based and to replace the norm-referenced GCE 'O' levels. The National Curriculum 5–16, the Scottish National Certificate, National Vocational Qualifications (NVQs) and General National Vocational Qualifications (GNVQs) are all designed to be broadly criterion-referenced.

Wolf (1993) identifies a number of advantages to this approach. She believes this method can improve teaching and learning; make assessment results comprehensible and useful and provide an opportunity for everyone to have their positive achievements recognised.

Learners need to know what is expected of them and what they need to do to succeed. Explicit criteria can provide this. If students do not succeed, of course, they need to know *which* criteria they have not met. Although in recent years it has been common practice to make learners aware of the assessment criteria, many marking schemes in the past remained 'secret' to the learner, especially – though not exclusively – in public examinations.

Figure 19 provides an example of formative feedback given to a student on a teaching course for the post-compulsory education and training (PCET) sector, after an observed lesson.

Note how this feedback, following marking, relates directly to the assessment criteria in Figure 18.

a) **a professional approach to the preparation and planning of teaching**
Your lesson plan is detailed, with appropriate aims and learning outcomes. The assessment strategies are appropriate. The activities are innovative and the timings are generally realistic. Your learning resources are beautifully prepared. However, is it practical to copy them for all your students?

Continued...

b) coherence and appropriate organisation in the scheme of work
The scheme of work relates well to the syllabus. It is realistic, clear and the topics are logically sequenced. You might, however, need more time allocated within the scheme for in-class assessment. It is not clear from the scheme exactly how much time will be allocated for the tasks.

c) competence in the delivery of the session
Your session was successful. Learning outcomes were met. Your style was relaxed and confident. You demonstrated good classroom management skills and you ensured that ALL learners were involved in the activity. Your writing on the whiteboard could be neater (keep practising!) and be careful not to have your back to the group for too long. One possibility would have been to ask one of the students to record the feedback on the whiteboard, leaving you free to manage the discussion.

d) evidence of the ability to reflect on own performance and to respond positively to constructive feedback
In your evaluation you have reflected thoughtfully on your performance. You have tended, however, to focus on the areas for improvement (what you call weaknesses). It is important to think, too, about your strengths. You need to know what it is you did to make things go well. Remember all the positive comments from your peers and tutor!

Overall - a very good lesson. All criteria met. Well done

Figure 19   An example of marking according to given criteria

Criteria are generally written by tutors (as in this example) or by those working for awarding bodies. There are many benefits, however, to encouraging students to devise their own criteria, either independently or in groups. This is discussed further in relation to self- and peer-assessment later in this section.

In *National Vocational Qualifications* (NVQs) the broad areas of competence are broken down into 'sub-areas', entitled *units*. Units are then divided into *elements of competence*. These elements are then broken down still further into *performance criteria*, which represent the fine detail of the activity. This might seem complex, but an example will make it clear.

Figures 20 and 21 are related to a qualification for dental nurses.

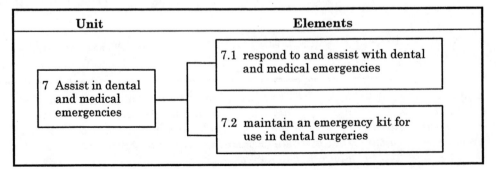

Figure 20   An example of a unit and two related elements

This shows just one of many units within the area of competence. Like other units it includes elements, and in this particular case there are two elements. The performance criteria for first of these elements are shown in Figure 21.

Element	Performance criteria
7.1 respond to and assist with dental and medical emergencies	a) the patient is reassured throughout by verbal and non-verbal means b) immediate/preliminary action is taken appropriate to the medical/dental condition c) the patient's pulse, temperature and breathing are monitored d) medical assistance is called for e) the patient's dignity is respected throughout

Figure 21   An example of an element and the related performance criteria

The candidate, as with all such models, is required to provide evidence to support claims of competence for this and other elements. Ideally, this is achieved in the workplace. If this is not possible, simulations are set up and the candidate is interviewed. The candidate collects evidence to support a claim of competence, usually in a *portfolio*, a method of assessment which is discussed in Section 10.

Criterion-referenced assessment has its drawbacks, too. Criteria may be unclear or ambiguous. They are not easy to write and this is particularly the case where aesthetic judgement by the tutor is required (see Section 10 in relation to creative arts and artefacts). Despite the use of criteria, assessment can remain subjective.

Those who design the assessment tasks may fail to agree on the criteria and, in marking the work or performance, assessors may interpret the criteria in different ways. Using the criteria in Figure 18, for example, assessors may not fully agree on what is meant by 'professional' in the first criterion. These problems, however, are normally resolved by a process of moderation or verification, as we discuss later in Section 9. There may be a wide variation in terms of the quality of work which might meet the specified criteria – excellent, good, sound and barely satisfactory. In some subjects, such as maths or the sciences, there will be answers which can be either right or wrong. In other subjects, there are shades of grey. The differences between levels of work was discussed in the previous section in relation to shades or levels of competence.

One method of recognising 'more than just competent' or 'easily meets the criteria' is to give some form of classification. Sometimes additional criteria are included for a Merit and for a Distinction. They may look something like this:

In order to gain a merit, all the criteria for a pass must be met and, in addition, the work must show ...

In order to gain a distinction, all the criteria for a merit must be met and, in addition, the work must show ...

Another method of classifying passes, used most frequently in higher education, is to link a numerical grade or percentage to specific criteria, as in Figure 22.

Write a review of a book of your choice for your professional journal.

0-29%	Does not constitute an answer to the question.
30-39%	Lacks many of the characteristics of a book review. Gives inadequate information about the book.
40-49%	Has basic characteristics of a book review. Gives information about book being reviewed.
50-59%	Has characteristics of a book review. Gives information about book being reviewed. Has adequate evaluation.
60-69%	Has characteristics of a book review. Gives information about book being reviewed. Evaluates the book being reviewed and judges its suitability for the readership of the journal.
70+%	Suitable for publication for the journal: is informative, evaluative, creative and interesting.

Figure 22   A set of criteria for writing a book review

(Gibbs, Habeshaw & Habeshaw, 1988a: 115)

With this example it may be hard for a teacher to explain why one student gets 52% and another gets 58% if both learners meet the criterion linked to that range of grades (50%–59%). Some tutors are very fond of this method of marking and will claim that they 'know a 52% when they see it'. In effect, they are probably operating a combination of norm-referenced and criterion-referenced assessment.

One of the problems with criteria is that there may also be *hidden* criteria. Teachers may, for example, dislike errors in grammar, spelling or punctuation. The use – or misuse – of the apostrophe is a particular favourite! While they may admit to themselves and to colleagues that this might influence their view of a student's work, teachers may not give feedback as no reference is made in the criteria. Students may remain unaware of this. This situation can be avoided, of course, by informing students and, if appropriate, making explicit any hidden criteria.

It is important to remember that the terms criterion-referenced and norm-referenced refer to the *type* of assessment, whereas the terms summative, formative and diagnostic, discussed in an earlier section, refer to the *purpose* of assessment.

In practice, the relationships between these terms is not always clear cut. Although criterion-referenced assessments are usually based on a pass or fail system, tutors still compare students' work and they also tend to have in their mind a certain number of students who they expect will pass or fail, based on their experience of previous years and maybe on departmental or organisational norms. It should be noted, too, that norm-referenced tests do have criteria – if only to establish the norm.

Alternatives to assessment by tutors

Assessment is most frequently undertaken by tutors or trainers and by external examiners and assessors. This need not always be the case though. Here are some alternative models.

Self-assessment

Self-assessment is a valuable form of assessment for learners. It can enable students to 'own' their learning. The simplest form of self-assessment is to ask students to mark their own work. They need not share the results with anyone else. There are, however, various ways in which self-assessment can be more formal. Trainees may be required, for example, to keep a reflective diary in which they chart the progress of their own learning and this form of assessment is discussed in Section 10. Self-assessment encourages learners to be reflective.

Self-assessment questions (SAQs), used in many Open University materials, provide a useful way in which learners can check their understanding or progress. SAQs pose questions for the reader to reflect on. If appropriate, answers are then provided. Although designed for distance learning modes of study, they can also be used effectively within a class or workplace environment at all levels. Figure 23 provides an example of an SAQ for you, as a reader of this particular book.

Read the first pages of this section again (pp79–85). Now write down in your own words what you think the terms **criterion-referenced** and **norm-referenced** mean. Check your descriptions with those we have given. Have you understood these two terms?

Figure 23   An example of a self-assessment question (SAQ)

Peer-assessment

Assessment can also be undertaken by peers. Students may mark each other's work or judge each other's performance. *Peer-assessment* is becoming increasingly popular. It may involve students in marking each other's work using given criteria or devising their own. Peer-assessment does not necessarily involve students in passing or failing their colleagues. It often requires the group to provide feedback after some type of presentation. This in turn can help students with their own self-assessment and reflection.

Many people find it difficult to assess their peers. Often, we do not want to be too critical and we may be concerned that any criticism will ruin a good relationship. The role of the teacher or facilitator is crucial, in giving guidelines to the group, outlining the process and explaining the benefits that can be drawn from taking part in assessing each other's work.

Race, who is very keen on student-devised criteria and on self- and peer-assessment, comments (1993: 51):

> *Where it is possible to draw assessment criteria from learners themselves, especially in group situations, the sense of ownership which learners develop is very powerful, and leads to them using the criteria with considerable enthusiasm and commitment when self- or peer-assessing.*

He goes on to describe the many tangible benefits for students and focuses on the processes involved. These include identifying criteria, discussing work with colleagues, making judgements and facilitating discussion in relation to fairness and objectivity.

Employer, client or sponsor assessment

In Section 7 we spoke about the many stakeholders who have an interest in the learning outcomes of others. There are many examples of when it is helpful to involve these people in assessment. Where a student is undertaking a project for a client within his or her own workplace, for example, it may be appropriate for the work to be assessed by the client.

Some competence-based programmes, like NVQs, as discussed earlier, are assessed in the workplace by assessors but the underpinning knowledge is 'delivered' and assessed by teachers at educational establishments.

NVQs require competence to be demonstrated in a 'realistic environment', i.e. the workplace, and ideally it is the employer who assesses, usually by observing and questioning the candidate while he or she is at work. Students completing NVQs in a college, however, may have to be assessed by their tutors while they are on work placement or when they are at college, 'working' in a simulated environment, such as a hairdressing salon, training office or training restaurant.

When learners on a business studies course present a business plan for a new venture they are planning, for example, assessment by a local bank manager may be invaluable. This element of 'real life' assessment can contribute significantly to learners' motivation.

However, despite the benefits of self-, peer- or 'outsider'-assessment, it is not unusual for students to feel more comfortable being assessed by the 'expert' teacher. They may believe that teacher assessment is more likely to be fair.

9.   Considerations of Fairness

In considering the fairness or unfairness of assessment in this section, we will examine three key concepts – *validity, reliability* and *utility*. We will then go on to discuss other factors affecting fairness and conclude by looking at some of the principles of *quality assurance*.

Validity

Validity is the extent to which a test measures what it is supposed to measure. A tape-measure is a valid tool for the measurement of length. It is not valid for measuring weight.

There is little point in conducting any kind of assessment unless tutors can be reasonably sure about what they are trying to measure. If you were assessing how well a student on an office technology programme could answer the telephone, for example, a written essay on telecommunications would not be an appropriate form of assessment. A role-play is likely to be a more valid form of assessment in this particular case.

It is clearly necessary to ensure that what is chosen for testing is representative of what the learner has learnt. Before deciding on the form and techniques of assessment, therefore, it is necessary to define educational aims and objectives for the learning which is to be assessed.

In your own teaching you will be aware of the importance of planning your sessions carefully. During the planning process you will be identifying learning outcomes for your students and also thinking about how you will check whether or not your learners have met these outcomes.

If we look at a section of a lesson plan (Figure 24, overleaf, taken again from the numeracy example we have considered in detail before) we will see that the assessment methods relate directly to the learning outcomes and that the tutor will be able to check whether or not these outcomes have been met.

Assessment techniques work best where learning outcomes have been clearly articulated in advance and, ideally, shared with learners.

The validity of an assessment may be affected by how well the learner has been prepared. It is not just a case of how much they have revised or how much work they have done in class. The feeling conveyed by tutors about the significance and importance of the assessment, as well as all the practical information about rooms and times, is also critical.

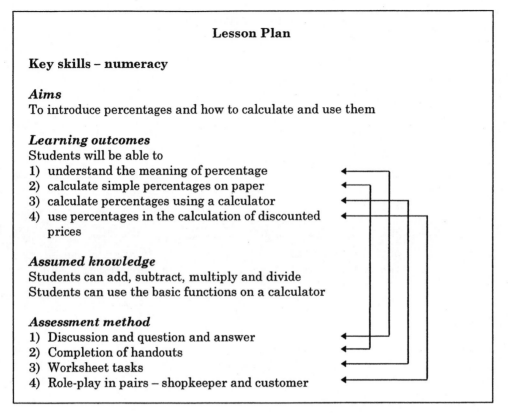

Figure 24   Part of a lesson plan

In terms of validity, there are other issues, such as face, content and criterion-related validity.

Face validity

Sometimes validity can be superficial and this is often referred to as face validity. Questionnaires in magazines, for example, may claim to tell readers about their personalities and presume to conclude that someone is a 'fast living extrovert with a taste for adventure'. Comments like these may tell people something about themselves but they do not really measure personalities.

Content validity

Content validity refers to how well any assessment process samples and measures accurately the knowledge and skills specified in the objectives of the lesson, module or unit. Tests can only sample some of the total possible items which may be included. For true content validity a test must adequately sample the relevant field of knowledge. This is an issue we will return to when we discuss the advantages and disadvantages of examinations. Exams often do not have high content validity. This is because students can pass exams even if they are very selective about what they revise and so they can ignore large proportions of the relevant subject matter.

To return yet again to the analogy of the practical driving test, it would be like allowing people to pass the test even if they had chosen to exclude some parts of the learning, for example, turning right or using indicators.

Criterion-related validity

Criterion-related validity relates to two of the prime purposes for which some tests are constructed – selection and estimation. It may be defined as the extent to which test performance is related to some other valued measure of performance. Some examples may help to clarify this.

Selection – Tests are often constructed with the intention of predicting future performance, but the extent to which they do so is largely a matter of statistical correlation. The 11+ examination, for example, was intended to be an indicator of a pupil's future academic suitability. Where a comparison of test results with some future performance is undertaken (e.g. A level results and final degree classifications) the term 'predictive validity' is often used.

Estimation – This concerns making estimates of present status. A Spanish vocabulary test, for example, might be used to estimate students' current skill in actual conversation in the language. This is often known as 'concurrent validity'.

Reliability

Reliability refers to the consistency of measurement. It refers to the extent to which an assessment will produce the same pattern of scores with the same population of students on two different occasions. However, we cannot expect test results to be perfectly consistent. There are a range of factors which may affect reliability.

If a test is administered to the same group twice in close succession, we might expect some variation in grades on the second occasion due to ill health, stress, inattention or any other reason. Nevertheless, the same general trend in the pattern of test scores should be detectable and, unless the measurement can be shown to be reasonably consistent over different occasions, we will not be able to place much confidence in the results.

With a long time-gap between testing, we may well see marked variation in an individual student's scores. Indeed, we may expect such a 'pay off' if a student has undertaken extra work or received more attention from the tutor.

Teachers normally establish pragmatically the reliability of the assessment measures which they use. They may, for example, look at assignment grades, note a shift in rank order amongst their students and then concern themselves with determining the reasons for any changes.

At a national level, there is a strong argument for seeking reliable end-of-course measures of student achievement. There is much debate, for example, about the reliability of degree classifications. Is a 2:1 (Upper Second) from one university equivalent to a 2:1 from another?

In many organisations, the notion of reliability in assessment is being replaced by the concept of quality assurance, which emphasises the need for procedures within organisations which are designed to ensure that assessments are as fair, reliable and valid as possible. This is discussed more fully below.

Utility

Earlier it was maintained that assessing learning should be a part of the teaching process and not just an afterthought. There are, however, also practical problems that relate to any form of assessment and these must be taken into consideration.

Assessments need to be:

- easily administered
- cost effective to produce and mark
- easily scored against well-understood criteria
- meaningfully interpreted and the results effectively applied in the context of the students' learning needs.

With formative assessment, the principles listed above usually present fewer problems. The devices we use involve little cost, although the greatest cost, of course, is tutors' time. In the case of summative assessment, however, the costs of producing certain assessment tasks may be high. Furthermore, their interpretation and application to students' learning needs may take some time to take effect. Discussion of the results and appropriate remedial work may not be immediately possible.

Factors affecting fairness

Physical or emotional factors

We are probably all familiar with the concept of 'exam nerves' or 'interview nerves'. Some students will perform less well under time constraints or when they know they are being formally assessed. During a workplace assessment, for example, trainees may become less proficient and confident than they would normally be owing to the pressure of the situation. Physical or emotional problems may prevent students from doing their best.

Assessor problems

The tutor may be unfamiliar with a particular programme or method of assessment. She or he may express a bias, either in favour or against a student, based on previous knowledge of the learner or on prejudices. Blind marking is sometimes used to avoid assessor bias. With blind marking students are given a number as a form of identification and therefore when the tutor marks the work, he or she does not know the name of the student. However, this method is only appropriate with written assessments and when large numbers of students are involved.

Differences may exist between assessors in their interpretation of the criteria. This may be because of variations in subject knowledge or degrees of confidence in making a judgement. If differences exist, they should be identified by the *verifier* or *moderator* as part of the organisation's quality assurance and control systems, as discussed below.

Inequalities

Learners may be unfairly penalised if they are assessed in a language which is not their first language. If a certain standard of written or spoken language is required, it should be stated in the criteria and students should be made aware of this and fully prepared.

Materials used for assessment purposes, for example, may be overtly Euro-centric and therefore discriminate against those students who are not European.

The language of assessment itself – whatever the students' first language – can also be a barrier. There is a bewildering amount of jargon surrounding assessment, much of which you may be struggling with yourself! Learners may be presented with not just tasks but also with a language which is alien to them.

Insufficient resources may also be a cause of unfair assessment. Tasks which require the use of the Internet, for example, may favour those learners who have access to the appropriate technology at home or at work.

Can assessment ever be fair? Gipps (1995: 279) suggests that:

> *There is no such thing as a fair test, nor could there be: the situation is too complex and the notion simplistic. However, by paying attention to what we know about factors in assessment, administration and scoring, we can begin to work towards tests that are more fair to all groups likely to be taking them, and this is particularly important for assessment used for summative and accountability purposes.*

Quality assurance

Several mentions have been made of moderators or quality assurance systems. Let us now look at this topic in more detail.

Most organisations involved in education and training have systems in place to avoid the kinds of barriers to fairness discussed above, as part of their quality assurance and quality control policies. This was mentioned above in relation to reliability. There are usually systems of internal moderation or verification, whereby tutors and assessors check each others' marking. In many cases, students' work is marked twice. Internal moderators or verifiers within an organisation may sample a range of work from different tutors. They offer advice and support to assessors and act as a link between the assessors and the awarding bodies.

There are also external moderators, verifiers and examiners. External moderators and verifiers are usually employed by the awarding or examining body. By visiting a range of institutions offering their particular programme or examination, they are able to comment on comparability of standards. They are also involved in ensuring that the assessment process is operated fairly and according to approved procedures and regulations.

External examiners, favoured by the higher education sector, have a similar role but they are usually employed by universities and they normally work on courses similar to the one they are examining.

Those responsible for assessment within NVQ programmes are usually qualified to what were formerly the *Training and Development Lead Body* (TDLB) standards. (The work of this, and the other Lead Bodies, has now been transferred to the new National Training Organisations, NTOs.) This means that the assessors themselves have undergone assessment. They have had to demonstrate that they can make judgements regarding the assessment of competence, which they have collected from a variety of sources.

Assessment policies, and detailed procedures for students who wish to appeal against an assessment decision, provide another safeguard for learners.

10.   Methods of Assessment

So far we have briefly mentioned a number of different ways of carrying out assessment, such as oral questioning, portfolios and examinations. There are, of course, many other methods and in this section we look at the main advantages and some of the drawbacks of different types of assessment.

The list of assessment methods below is not exhaustive but it does demonstrate a wide variety of possibilities:

- examinations
- essays
- objective tests
- projects and reports
- observation
- portfolios
- diaries and log books
- creative arts and artefacts
- questioning, interviews, orals and role-play
- problem-solving tasks
- computer-based assessment.

These methods will now be discussed in an attempt to highlight their strengths and weaknesses.

Examinations

It is often argued that written exams are the most efficient form of assessment. All the students sit them at the same time and there is little chance of plagiarism. The scripts can be marked relatively quickly by tutors, who will, in theory, have finished their teaching.

Exams do have advantages. The fact that summative exams play a key role in motivating students should not be underestimated. They can provide a stimulus for students. 'I didn't really understand this course until I started revising for the exams; then it all clicked into place' is not an unusual sentiment. This statement, of course, is more of an indictment of the teaching and learning, than an advantage of examinations as a form of assessment! However, exams can effectively test a learner's factual knowledge and his or her ability to work swiftly and under pressure.

Unfortunately, they can also encourage last minute cramming and a surface approach to learning. Students can regurgitate facts without understanding them. Exams also offer students the opportunity to exclude large sections of the curriculum they have been studying and to concentrate on questions they think will 'come up'.

The fact that the same exam paper is taken by a large number of people does not necessarily make it a valid or reliable form of assessment. In fact, if students have extensive choice within an exam, it can mean, in effect, that no two students sit the same paper. A large number of short questions would lead to greater reliability than asking students to choose just three topics out of fifteen. If students are not required to show an understanding of *all* aspects of a course – which is usually the case in exams – it means that the assessment is invalid, as we discussed in relation to content validity. There are also many issues relating to fairness, as we saw earlier. Some students get very nervous before and during exams. Other students have developed – or have been coached in – good exam techniques.

Not all examinations need follow a traditional format which starts with 'You may now turn over your papers'. There are advantages to experimenting with the format. Exams may have a flexible time constraint. This may, for example, mean giving students a whole day or even week to complete a piece of work. Trainees may be given a case study to read a week before the exam. On the day of the exam they can be given the questions which relate to the case study.

Other formats include giving learners questions they have had a chance to prepare for (seen papers) or allowing them to use their notes and other texts (open-book) during an exam. They may also be given exam papers to take away and complete at home.

Essays

Essays remain a common form of assessment for many 'academic' programmes, particularly in the arts and social sciences and especially on higher education courses. They may be very useful ways of assessing learning in that students are given an opportunity to demonstrate an ability to integrate knowledge, skills and understanding. Essay writing should be about trying out ideas and arguments supported by evidence.

There are, however, many problems with using essays as a form of assessment. Learners need first of all to acquire the skill of *how* to write an essay. In gathering evidence, there is a temptation for students to copy large sections from books (or from other students' work). Essays can be difficult to mark objectively, which is why it is essential to clarify the criteria and make them available to students, as we discussed earlier.

Objective tests

As the name suggests, *objective tests* are a type of assessment in which the marking is objective. Unlike essays, the answers to objective tests are predetermined. Marking the answer to a question like 'What is the capital of Japan?', for example, requires little in the way of subjective judgement. It is important to note, though, that the subjectivity is eliminated only in the marking and that it can remain in the setting. Let us look at the example in Figure 25, from a Level 1 NVQ Hairdressing question paper.

Choosing the correct shampoo usually depends on:

a)   what the client asks for

b)   the salon stock

c)   the client's hair type

d)   the condition of the client's hair.

Figure 25 An example of a multiple-choice question

In this example, the marking is objective, in that the person setting the test has identified the 'correct' answer, but there is clearly an element of subjectivity in the setting of the questions.

Multiple-choice questions, as in Figure 25, are just one type of objective test. Others require learners to:

- choose between A and B
- tick TRUE or FALSE for the following statements ...
- complete the following sentences ...
- identify the missing word in each sentence ...
- match the items in one column with the items in the second column (for example, events in one column and dates they took place in the other)
- select the best answer from the following ...

Objective tests have many advantages:

- they can be marked easily by tutors;
- they can be marked quickly by tutors;
- they can be marked by optical bar-code readers or scanners;
- they can be marked by someone who is not an expert in the subject;
- they can be very reliable, in that all tutors involved will be marking to the same standard;
- a greater proportion of the syllabus can be covered than in other forms of assessment;
- students are required to answer all questions;
- they can effectively test factual knowledge;
- in some cases, they can test more than just facts, as described below.

Brown & Knight (1994) argue that multiple-choice papers can effectively test higher cognitive skills, such as comprehension, analysis, synthesis, interpretation and reasoning. They describe a 'best answer' paper for medical students where a question comprises a brief description of a patient and the presenting symptoms. The trainee doctor is required to select the most appropriate prescription from a selection of several. More than one of the alternatives may be acceptable and experts would have to agree that one of them is the best and that it should get more marks than the others which are possible. Those that are inappropriate would score no marks or possibly negative marks.

While objective tests may be useful as one part of an overall assessment strategy, there are drawbacks to this approach. The main problem is the design of the questions, which need to be absolutely clear and unambiguous. If they are poorly designed then the assessment is not valid. There may also be problems about students guessing the answers, although many papers are designed to penalise guessing by deducting marks for the wrong answer. The over-use of this method can make learning routine and trivialise the answers. Although objective tests can be used to assess higher cognitive skills, they tend to be used primarily for factual recall, and they cannot assess creativity.

Projects and reports

Projects and reports can take many forms and they can be undertaken by individuals or in groups. They enable learners to explore in depth a particular topic. If students have chosen their own title or topic, it is likely to provide them with a form of ownership of the learning.

These tasks can foster independence and creative problem solving. They can also help learners develop project and time management skills as well as those skills relating to research, information-seeking and team-working. Realistic tasks, related to the working environment, combined with continuous assessment can be a more attractive assessment option than essays or exams for many students.

In terms of disadvantages, there is a possibility of time constraints, especially if it is difficult to meet the requirements of an externally set syllabus in the time allocated. There may also be problems with plagiarism and, with groupwork, there are issues relating to the recognition of each individual's contribution. Maintaining reliability in terms of marking may also be a cause for concern. All these problems, though, can be avoided to a large extent by providing appropriate criteria, a clear brief and a system of moderation.

Observation

Observation is about watching students and noting what you see. It can be a very effective way of establishing if learning has taken place and it is particularly useful for assessing processes, as discussed in Section 7. Teachers informally observe their learners, of course, all the time in a classroom, workshop or workplace environment. If processes are being assessed, then it is important to make sure that this is made clear in the criteria. An art tutor, for example, may be assessing not just a completed piece of work (the product) but also the way in which the learner worked through the design stages, met project deadlines or possibly worked with others.

Observation is frequently used for competence-based assessment, to observe learners in a 'real' working environment. It is usual practice, when undertaking such an observation, for the tutor to have either a checklist or a standard form to complete. This system has advantages. If the checklist is carefully thought out, in advance of the observation, it is likely to cover the relevant aspects to be observed and this can help to ensure the validity of the assessment. It provides a simple means of recording the observation. Using the same checklist for each observation (for the same or different learners) can also increase the reliability of the assessment, particularly if more than one assessor is involved.

Assessment by observation can be motivating for the learner. It can reinforce theory, certify competence and provide an 'I can do' feel-good factor.

Some of the drawbacks of observation as a method of assessment are identified below.

- In the design of a checklist it is difficult to include *all* possible situations and some features will inevitably be omitted. Forms with broad headings allow greater scope for the assessor but may reduce reliability or validity.

- Sufficiency of evidence may prove to be a problem. You may need to observe someone several times (if time permits) to be confident about their abilities and competence.

- There may be bias on the part of the assessor. Some trainees may be given the benefit of the doubt whereas others in a similar situation may not.

- The presence of an observer will change the environment. The candidate may feel nervous and act differently. Other people involved may also behave in an unusual manner.

Portfolios

A portfolio is a documentary record or a collection of evidence. Traditionally used by art students to demonstrate their achievements, the term 'portfolio' is now applied to a whole range of subject areas, at varying levels and in different modes of work or study.

Portfolio compilers may be young people on a vocational course at school or college, collating their coursework or, as noted by Bloor & Butterworth (1996), they may be employees planning their career route through a company, students recording their period of study on a training course or applicants to a college or university putting together a claim for the *accreditation of prior learning* (APL). The advantages of this approach are that it can:

- provide a 'portable record' of someone's achievements or professional experience
- encourage people to take responsibility for their learning and for their assessment
- be a particularly effective method of claiming APL
- help employees to plan their career development
- encourage people to be reflective.

Sometimes, however, learners find the prospect of compiling a portfolio daunting. They may have difficulty in interpreting the language and jargon associated with portfolios, especially in relation to performance criteria. It can be the case that where students in colleges are required to compile a portfolio, learning is overly assessment-driven. Teachers and students can become so concerned with the mechanics of portfolios and their presentation that this overshadows their purpose and the related learning processes and educational outcomes.

Those claiming APL for the purpose of exemption from part of a programme (for example, one unit) may find that completing the unit in the traditional way is actually easier and less time-consuming than putting together a portfolio.

Diaries and log books

Diaries and log books provide a personal record of experiences. The former tend to be more subjective than the latter but both focus on the process of learning. They are often used alongside other forms of assessment. They may, for example, be used to record experiences whilst on work placement, undertaking a science practical or working in a team on a group project. When we discussed projects earlier, it was noted that marking groupwork assignments can be problematic.

One method of improving this type of assessment is to require each member of the group to keep a diary or log, outlining their own contribution. Diaries are a form of self-assessment; they encourage learners to make reflections on their experience or their behaviour in specific situations. They can provide evidence of process for a tutor to assess. It is possible, though, that in some cases students may not be honest or may not recognise this method as a suitable type of assessment.

Creative arts and artefacts

The competence-based approach is at its most controversial in relation to the assessment of the creative arts. Many would argue that providing learners with explicit criteria is likely to stifle their creativity. However, guidance in the form of criteria does remove the unfairness of a system whereby students are expected to guess what is in the mind of the assessor. Brown & Knight (1994) argue that the mystery surrounding assessment of the creative arts stems from the old master/apprenticeship relationship in which the master had the power to decide whether the apprentice's achievement was aesthetically pleasing or not. Overt and clear criteria can provide the necessary guidelines for technical competence, techniques, time scales and use of materials.

However, even with these criteria, there will remain an element of subjectivity in the assessment of any 'final' product, be it a ceramic bowl, a painting, a hairstyle, a chair, a poem or a meal. It is important for tutors to recognise this element of subjectivity and be open and honest with students in their feedback.

Questioning, interviews, orals and role-play

Oral question and answer is frequently used for formative assessment of students' learning. The main advantage of this type of assessment is its immediacy, which is why it is popular with teachers in the classroom setting. It is normally used in conjunction with other methods of assessment. Its success depends to a large extent on the skill of the teacher. Teachers have to ensure that questions are appropriate, that they test understanding and not just factual recall and that they are answered by all students and not just a few dominant ones. Teachers often ask 'Are there any questions – anything you don't understand?' but sometimes fall into the trap of assuming that students' silence equates to students' understanding.

Interviews are sometimes used to contribute towards summative assessment. This may be the case, for example, with candidates submitting a piece of work or a portfolio. The interview can be used to confirm that the candidate is the author of the work and to explore certain issues in more depth. This is similar to the use of vivas in colleges and universities for doctorate students or for students who are borderline in terms of their grades.

In preparing students for finding employment, mock interviews can assess learners' personal qualities and attitudes and interpersonal skills, particularly if used with a check-list of characteristics.

Oral exams and role-play exercises tend to be associated with language learning. In this context, they can very effectively assess fluency and comprehension. Role-plays can also be used at all levels on a wide range of programmes to assess students' ability to think quickly and react in an appropriate way to varying situations. Students can be given a scenario and then asked to act it out, either with each other, or with an examiner or teacher. A student on a travel and tourism course, for example, may be required to demonstrate how he or she would react to a very awkward and unpleasant customer or holidaymaker. Law students may be required to act out scenes in a court to assess their negotiating skills and knowledge of the law.

Clearly, these forms of assessment have many advantages. One-to-one interviews and oral exams enable the questioner to explore understanding and pick up issues not covered in a student's written work. Oral exams and role-plays are very practical, 'real life' forms of assessments and, as such, students will appreciate their relevance.

However, these types of 'on the spot' situations can also be very stressful for some students. Although there are likely to be criteria for passing or failing, the assessment can appear to be very subjective, which raises questions about reliability. There may also be practical problems related to arranging orals, interviews or role-plays for large numbers of students within a limited time frame.

Problem-solving tasks

This is a broad heading for a wide range of activities, which can take many forms. Problem-solving tasks are often related to practical assignments which take into account commercial pressures and practices. A day-long in-tray assessment, for example, may require students on an office technology course to read all the papers in their 'tray'. They then have to scan through all the documents, prioritise the tasks and complete those that need to be finished by the end of that day. Clearly this type of assessment can assess some working competences more effectively than a written exam.

Mini-enterprise tasks are of a similar nature. Students on business studies programmes may be required to set up their own business to raise money. These assessments can continue throughout a term, semester or even a whole academic year. Students may, for example, offer a car cleaning service to colleagues and staff. In doing so they need to write a business plan, design, print and distribute leaflets, organise 'staffing' schedules and training as well as keep the accounts. Such activities provide the opportunity to assess not just business knowledge but also interpersonal and team working skills. They can very effectively demonstrate how students have related theory to practice. This type of assessment can be very time-consuming to arrange and to monitor for the tutors involved and, particularly if students take on different roles within their team, criteria for assessment have to be made very clear to ensure reliability and validity.

Some problem-solving tasks are computer-based. Simulations, for example, enable students to experiment with different variables to see the effect this has on certain situations.

Computer-based assessment

Technology is used in all sorts of way to assist in assessment. Optical mark scanners or readers are used in the marking of objective tests, as noted earlier in this section. Computers are, of course, also used to create assignments as well as to record, analyse and communicate results. Feedback tutorials are increasingly undertaken, as we saw earlier, by email, electronic or video conferencing.

There are software packages available which enable learners to respond to questions on the computer screen. Tutors can write their own banks of questions at different levels. Banks of questions for some syllabi – notably GCSE and A levels – are sold commercially. On most systems, multimedia resources such as sound or video can be brought in to present a test or give feedback on answers. The responses of the students are stored and collated automatically. The system can provide students with instant feedback and it is generally easy to use. Tutors may, of course, have to spend time initially devising the questions. Appropriate computing facilities are necessary for each student, although not all students have to take the assessments at the same time.

It is important not to be overawed by the technology and to remember that these objective tests can have the same drawbacks and limitations as the manual versions and can lead to a surface approach to learning.

Computers are also used to provide simulations of events which could not be otherwise simulated. Assessments can be designed around these simulations. Gibbs, Habeshaw & Habeshaw (1988a) describe a computer simulation of the economy. A desired economic state for five years from now is specified and today's economic indicators are input at the beginning of the session. Students are then set the task of achieving this desired state by manipulating those variables within the control of, say, the Chancellor of the Exchequer. With this, as with other simulations, students explore a variety of 'what if...' scenarios.

Advances in technology will no doubt continue to facilitate more 'real life' assessment. Virtual reality is already used in teaching and training in some institutions. It places a person into a simulated environment that looks and feels to some degree like the real world. People in this synthetic environment can move their head and eyes to explore it, feel the space that surrounds them and can interact with the objects in it. Simulated objects appear solid: they can be picked up, examined from all sides, navigated around, heard, touched and explored in many sensory ways.

Virtual reality has enormous potential in relation to teaching, learning and assessment. Using virtual reality systems it is possible for the learner to create images and objects which would take a long time to construct, or not be feasible to construct at all. Trainee architects – or their assessors – can walk around the buildings they design. Trainees in the printing industry can demonstrate their ability to operate expensive equipment without the risk of losing vast sums of money for their employers if they make a mistake. Those involved in the performing arts can use virtual reality for stage lighting and stage design courses.

Conclusion

We have discussed a diverse range of assessment strategies. All types have their strengths and weaknesses and it is likely that each method disadvantages some students in some way. It is preferable, therefore, for teachers and trainers to include in their repertoire a range of assessment methods. They will need to support educational aims, though the choices may be restricted because of resource or time constraints. Variety is as important for effective assessment as it is for all other aspects of teaching and learning.

References and Further Reading

All the publications cited or quoted from in the text are included in the following list.

Ashcroft K & Foreman-Peck L (1994) *Managing teaching and learning in further and higher education* Falmer Press

Barnes D (1971) *Language, the learner and the school* Penguin

Bloor M & Butterworth C (1996) 'The portfolio approach to professional development' in J Robson (ed) *The professional FE teacher* Avebury

Brown G & Pendlebury M (1992) *Assessing active learning* Committee of Vice-Chancellors and Principals Universities' Staff Development and Training Unit

Brown S, Jones G & Rawnsley S (1993) *Observing teaching* Staff and Educational Development Association

Brown S & Knight P (1994) *Assessing learners in higher education* Kogan Page

Curzon LB (1997) *Teaching in further education: an outline of principles and practice* 5th edn Cassell

Gibbs G, Habeshaw S, & Habeshaw T (1988a) *53 interesting ways to assess your students* 2nd edn Technical and Educational Services Ltd

Gibbs G, Habeshaw S & Habeshaw T (1988b) *53 interesting ways to appraise your teaching* Technical and Educational Services Ltd

Gipps C (1995) 'What do we mean by equity?' in *Assessment in education: principles, policy and practice* 2 (3)

Habeshaw S, Habeshaw T & Gibbs G (1992) *53 interesting things to do in your seminars and tutorials* Technical and Educational Services Ltd

Huddleston P & Unwin L (1997) *Learning and teaching in further education: diversity and change* Routledge

Huxley M (1987) 'Mismatch and disruption' in FEU *Behaviour and motivation: disruption in further education* Further Education Unit

Mansell J (1987) 'Introduction' in FEU *Behaviour and motivation: disruption in further education* Further Education Unit

Minton D (1997) *Teaching skills in further and adult education* 2nd edn Macmillan

Mitchell C (1997) *Transforming teaching: selecting and evaluating teaching strategies* FEDA

Nugent D (1996) 'Managing a learning situation' in N Zepke, D Nugent & SC Roberts (eds) *The new self-help book for teachers* Wellington: WP Press

Race P (1993) *Never mind the teaching feel the learning* Paper 80 Staff and Educational Development Association

Ramsden P (1992) *Learning to teach in higher education* Routledge

Reece I & Walker S (1997) *Teaching, training and learning* 3rd edn Business Education

Rogers A (1996) *Teaching adults* 2nd edn Open University Press

Rowntree D (1981) *Developing courses for students* Harper & Row

Rowntree D (1987) *Assessing students: how shall we know them?* 2nd edn Kogan Page

Slavin R E (1986) *Educational psychology: theory and practice* 4th edn Allyn & Bacon

Tannen D (1995) *Talking from 9 to 5* Virago

Wolf A (1993) *Assessment issues and problems in a criterion-based system* Further Education Unit

UDACE (1992) *Learning outcomes in higher education* Unit for the Development of Adult & Continuing Education

Further recommended reading

Anderson D, Brown S & Race P (1997) *500 tips for further and continuing education lecturers* Kogan Page

Ashcroft K (1996) *Researching into assessment and evaluation in colleges and universities* Kogan Page

Beech JR & Harding L (eds) (1990) *Testing people* Routledge

Ecclestone K (1996) *How to assess the vocational curriculum* Kogan Page

Further Education Unit (1992) *The assessment of prior learning and learner services* FEU

Jaques D (1991) *Learning in groups* Kogan Page

Peterson R (1998) *Training needs assessment* 2nd edn Routledge

Appendices

Appendix A

Verbs for writing outcomes/objectives

List of words commonly used when writing learning outcomes:

analyse	justify
assess	label
calibrate	list
categorise	measure
compare	name
compose	operate
construct	paint
convert	perform
define	predict
demonstrate	quantify
describe	recall
devise	recite
differentiate	relate
estimate	reproduce
explain	select
give examples	sketch
identify	solve
illustrate	state
indicate	summarise
interpret	use

Appendix B

Non-sexist language in teaching

The source of the following guidelines is:

The Open University (1997) *Adult learners, education and training (E827) Project and assignment guide* The Open University

The nature of language use is such that some of the terms listed below may come to be appropriated and misused. When this occurs terms are redefined, used differently or simply dropped from academic use. We urge you to make every effort to keep abreast of changes and to be sensitive to the use of various terms. In order to help you find alternatives to commonplace sexist language, we have prepared the following checklist:

To be avoided	To be preferred
mankind	humanity, human beings, human race, people, humankind, humans
man's achievements	human achievements, our achievements
if a man drove 50 miles at 60 mph	if a person drove 50 miles at 60 mph
the best man for the job	the best person (or candidate) for the job
man-made	artificial, synthetic, manufactured, constructed, of human origin
manpower	workers, workforce, staff, labour, staffing, human resources
man the desk	staff the desk, be at the desk
manpower planning	labour market planning, workforce, planning, staff planning, workload
chairman	chairperson, chair, convenor (don't use non-parallel terms, such as 'chairman' for men and 'chairperson' for women.
headmaster	headteacher, head
policeman	police officer

If the gender of the person being discussed is unknown or could be female or male, use s/he, she or her, he or she. However, since this may sound clumsy, you may prefer to use the plural where sense permits. Alternatively, you may decide that a pronoun is unnecessary.

To be avoided	To be preferred
man and his universe	humans and their universe
	humans and the universe
the consumer or shopper ... she	consumers or shoppers ... they
The secretary ... she	secretaries ... they
the breadwinner ... his earnings	breadwinners ... their earnings
	the breadwinner ... his or her earnings

Males should not always be first in order of mention. Alternate the order, sometimes using women and men, she or he, her or his. (But do not alternate in the same sentence or in the same paragraph as the result will sound awkward.)

These examples show ways of re-wording material to avoid sexism in language:

It is not very helpful to tell *someone that he is* insensitive unless you exemplify this.
(... people that they are ...)

This approach was criticised for suggesting that *man* is a passive agent.
(... an individual/the individual/is a passive agent / people are passive agents.)

A teacher may think it likely that *his* views will be accepted.
(... his or her / teachers may think it likely that their views will be accepted.)

... using such criteria as *chairmanship* or classroom skills.
(... classroom skills or the ability to chair a meeting.)

Here a good intention has been awkwardly put into practice:

He or she may have something or his on her mind.
(He or she may be worried about something.)